MARKETING
FINANCIAL
SERVICES

by
Robert C. Perez, Ph.D.

Associate Professor, Business Faculty,
Iona College, Hagan School of Business,
and Former Vice President and
Voting Stockholder, F. Eberstadt & Co., Inc.

PRAEGER

PRAEGER SPECIAL STUDIES • PRAEGER SCIENTIFIC

Library of Congress Cataloging in Publication Data

Perez, Robert C.
  Marketing financial services.

  Bibliography: p.
  Includes index.
  1. Financial institutions—United States.
2. Financial institutions—Marketing.   I. Title.
HG181.P39 1983   332.1′068′8   83-4230
ISBN 0-03-062452-5

Published in 1983 by Praeger Publishers
CBS Educational and Professional Publishing
a Division of CBS Inc.
521 Fifth Avenue, New York, NY 10175 USA

© 1983 by Praeger Publishers

3456789 052 987654321

Printed in the United States of America
on acid-free paper

Preface

The service sector of the economy has surpassed manufacturing as the principal economic activity in the private sector. This continues the trend, extending back over several decades, of the change of the United States from a goods producing economy to a provider of intangible services. J.-J. Servan-Schreiber, in his book, *The American Challenge*, describes this process as the evolution of a post-industrial society.

The financial service field is in the forefront of this evolving trend. According to the Commerce Department, financial institutions' profits after tax are growing more than two times faster than the profits of all U.S. nonfinancial institutions.[1] The financial services field at present is highly segmented and grossly over-regulated and it lacks the stimulation of marketing that has characterized the consumer goods industry. Nonetheless it is in the midst of a veritable revolution that seems sure to make financial services more readily available, cheaper, more highly competitive and less restrictive.

The Secretary of the Treasury, Donald Regan, recently described the impact that regulation has had on the financial services field.

"The result of (regulation) was a statutory framework that separates one class of depository institution from another, that proscribes bank mergers and acquisitions across certain geographic boundaries and that has balkanized our financial system into 42,000 depository institutions, including 15,000 commercial bankers." Regan recommends changing the regulation to permit limited nationwide branch systems based on Federal Reserve Districts. He concludes: "Market segmentation doesn't make sense now. Financial services have become more competitive and complex. Almost all of the previously specialized firms are trying to compete by moving into several niches (of the market place)."[2]

The ultimate goal of all this seems to be a people's capitalism in deed rather than word. One envisions making mutual fund investments, sorting out insurance needs, arranging for floating lines of credit, tending to credit card arrangements, exploring different avenues of financing for one's business, and perhaps receiving advice on the best stock investments — all at a financial "department store" conveniently located next to the hardware department at each of Sears, Roebuck and Co.'s 2,000 branch stores throughout the nation.

To be sure, it will be some time before this comes to pass — if ever. The consumer perceives the various financial services in different molds. He thinks that when he needs insurance advice he will get the best service by going to a specialist—the insurance agent. He uses a stock broker when he wants to buy stocks, a mutual fund when he wants to hire professionals to manage his stock investments, a banker when he wants to extend or enlarge his loan, and finally, a savings bank when he wants to refinance his home mortgage. These perceptions run deep in the American consumer conscience, nurtured by the years of restrictive regulations that have effectively segmented the financial service field into various sectors.

All of these services have one thing in common: they fall within that broad category of the financial field known as "financial intermediaries." Donald R. Fraser, a member of the business faculty of Texas A & M University, defines this term as follows:

> Financial intermediaries perform a number of services. These include providing a low risk outlet for the funds of individuals and businesses in the form of demand and time and savings deposits as well as in other financial instruments; assisting in fulfilling the credit or borrowing needs of the various sectors of the economy (consumer, business, and government); providing the mechanism for the payments and collections system of the United States, offering trust services; and providing a large variety of specific (miscellaneous) services necessary for the efficient operation of the business and financial system.... Financial intermediaries ... provide the following collective services: denomination intermediation, default risk intermediation, and maturity intermediation.

Fraser goes on to explain that the first of these refers to the ability of the financial intermediary to reduce the problems associated with lenders who require small allotments and businesses that prefer to issue securities in large denominations.

Financial intermediaries resolve this conflict by repackaging savings into larger amounts. The commercial banker, for example, makes large loans to...businesses...based on the savings and checking accounts of many individuals. In essence, the financial intermediary pools the savings of a large number of individuals and provides funds to a different group of borrowers.

The second vital function performed by financial intermediaries is default risk intermediation. Lenders are risk averse but many businesses can only offer securities which contain substantial...risks. Again there is a conflict between the preferences of lender and borrower. The financial intermediary reduces this conflict by purchasing the relatively high risk securities of businesses and, in turn, issuing its own securities which are relatively low risk. This is possible for a number of reasons. Through diversification of the assets in its portfolio the financial intermediary may be able to reduce the risk of its portfolio below the risk level on any of its individual assets. ...The financial intermediary should be able to employ individuals with specialized skill in order to appraise more accurately the degree of risk involved in the purchase of any given security. [Finally], deposit insurance has reduced the default risk of depository institutions—commercial banks, mutual savings banks, savings and loan associations, and credit unions.

Financial intermediaries also engage in the third function mentioned—maturity intermediation. Lenders prefer holding securities which can be converted into cash on relatively short notice. However, borrowers wish to issue relatively long-term securities. Financial intermediaries resolve these different maturity preferences by purchasing long-term securities and financing the purchase by issuing relatively short maturity securities. This is possible in the case of deposit institutions since the financial intermediary can expect that a substantial proportion of its deposit withdrawals will be offset by deposit inflow over any given period. ...The existence of maturity intermediation does however mean that all financial intermediaries are necessarily illiquid and subject to problems when facing large demands for funds from depositors. The plight of the savings and loan industry in periods of high interest rates [is an example] of this problem.

Financial intermediaries perform two other functions that are especially important. They may offer economies of scale in the lending and investing of funds, due to the specialized nature of the institution, so that savings may be made available to the ultimate investor at lower cost. Similarly, financial intermediaries may offer convenience to the investor in terms of physical location, record keeping, and the ability to shift from one investment to another quickly and with low transaction costs. The element of convenience may be especially important in the development of the management investment industry."[3]

The U.S. system of financial intermediaries varies considerably from the English and European financial service format. There a customer transacts most of his financial business at one location, usually a bank, which offers all of these arrangements. But then Americans do not accept the metric system despite its simplicity and widespread use throughout the western world.

This book will examine the possibilities for homogenizing financial services, now, and in the future. The book will analyze the marketing systems used for distributing financial services to consumers and industry. Emphasis will be placed on the historical development of the marketing of financial services and the evolution and adaptation of the "marketing concept" to a field characterized by regulatory and fiduciary relationships. The applications of advertising and promotion, selling, product development, distribution channels, pricing, and market research to the financial services field will be examined.

The author believes such a study is particularly useful at the present time. The financial service industry is in upheaval. Deregulation is increasing competition and forcing firms in this field to be innovative in their marketing programs and strategies.

The financial services industry ranks among the largest and most rapidly growing elements of the burgeoning service sector of the economy. New York has replaced London as the financial capital of the world. Accordingly, career opportunities abound in this rapidly growing field. Employment in the field of financial services continues to expand in the face of sluggish economic growth, volatile bond and stock markets, and a chaotic housing finance industry. It is hoped that this book will be useful to those who wish to pursue financial services as a career. To the author's knowledge, no marketing book exists to fill this void. This book should begin to fill that need and could lead to broader interest in the field.

U.S. industry faces huge capital investments to increase productivity and the ability to compete by the turn of the century. The exact amount of investment will ultimately depend on the price of energy and many other factors but the sums being talked about are staggering. The capital required could range from $40 billion to $80 billion a year, according to Richard C. Carlson, a senior economist with SRI International, a consulting firm in Menlo Park, California. Such a commitment would represent between one-quarter and one-half of all nonresidential fixed investment in the United States.[4]

The outlook for investment opportunities appears much more promising for the balance of the century than it did during the grim decade of the 1970s. Some forecasters project rates of return on equity investments will average 20 percent per annum for the rest of the century, three times the average return in the past ten years.

Finally, the author believes that the marketing of financial services differs considerably from the marketing of tangible consumer goods. As G. Lynn Shostack, vice president, marketing, for Citibank's Investment Management Group expressed it:

New concepts are necessary if service marketing is to succeed... Despite the increasing dominance of services in the U.S. economy, basic texts still disagree on how services should be treated in a marketing context." Shostack points out that marketing seems to be overwhelmingly product-oriented. Merely adopting product marketing's labels does not resolve the question of whether product marketing can be overlaid on service businesses. Can corporate banking services really be marketed according to the same basic blueprint that made *Tide* a success?

Shostack feels it is wrong to imply that services are just like products "except" for their intangibility.

By such logic, apples are just like oranges, except for their 'appleness'. ... [Intangibility is not a modifier, it is a state.] A service cannot be stored on a shelf, touched, tasted or tried on for size.

She concludes that marketing should attempt to associate the services with some form of tangible, concrete qualities.

Merrill Lynch, for instance, has firmly associated itself with a clear visual symbol of a bull and concomitant bullishness. The principle offered for marketers of services is that effective media representation of intangibles is a function of establishing non-abstract manifestations of them.[5]

PLAN OF THE BOOK

After an introductory chapter that brushes in the history and current state of the art of the financial services field the book will focus on several broad controversial issues that are at the center of heated debate in the field today, including:

- the impact of regulation on marketing activities in the financial service field and the current trend to deregulation
- the marketing concept and its adaptation to the financial service field-the conflict between the marketing concept and the fiduciary standard
- market and new product research in the financial service field
- "scrambled merchandising" between competitive financial service sectors to smooth out the volatile earnings and revenue swings that have, historically, been the bane of the business.

After this concentration on specific issues the author will examine in detail the marketing activities of each of the major sectors of the field. This examination will concentrate on the four "Ps" of marketing, product, price, place and promotion.[6] This examination will cover commercial banks, the savings industry, life and casualty insurance companies, mutual fund management companies, securities and investment banking concerns, and the pension fund management field.

NOTES

1. U.S. Department of Commerce, "National Income and Product Account of Industry, 1929-65 and Survey of Current Business."

2. "What's Wrong With Glass-Steagall." *Institutional Investor*, October 1981, pp. 21-22.

3. "The Money Market Fund, A Financial Intermediary," *MSU Business Topics* 25(2)(Spring 1977):5-11.

4. "American Industry Faces Huge Capital Investment to Increase Efficiency," *New York Times*, January 11, 1981.

5. "Breaking Free from Product Marketing", *Journal of Marketing*, April 1977, pp. 73-80.

6. E. Jerome McCarthy, *Basic Marketing: A Managerial Approach* (6th ed.) (Homewood, Ill.: Richard D. Irwin), pp. 38–43.

Contents

LIST OF TABLES AND FIGURE

Tables

Figure

ONE

Trends in the Financial Service Field

Marketing has descended on the financial service field with a vengeance. This new development in the world of finance has had its genesis in many sources. Gone are the days when the diverse sectors of the financial service field operated as virtual monopolies. Today banks, mutual funds, stock brokerages, insurance companies and thrift institutions compete ferociously with each other.

Once divided into separate market niches or sub-industries by type of service offered, the financial services industry today is changing. Boundary lines are beginning to blur and competition is becoming fierce. The biggest push is coming from the federal government that once maintained the separate and distinct nature of the industry but is now eroding protection by a new wave of deregulation. This deregulation trend will benefit most consumers and companies. A stronger and more unified industry will emerge as competition accelerates. Financial institutions will bear little resemblance to their former selves, but will offer business and the consumer a wider range of financing possibilities and services.

These changes are just in the beginning stages and therefore many financial service institutions do not yet perceive their extent or, at least, they do not acknowledge their pervasiveness or long-

1

range implications. Most securities firms and commercial banks, for example, tend to view themselves as being able to cope and exist as they always have. A few innovators, like Citicorp and Merrill Lynch, however, are placing themselves in a more strategic position to compete.

Complicating life a little further for these former fiefdoms of finance are the reckless outsiders, including chain stores, consumer credit companies, oil companies, travel companies and steel companies who see in the emerging world of financial services a panacea for their own growth problems. These entrées into the once highly segmented field of finance represent an upheaval the like of which has not been seen since the wave of regulation and restrictive legislation in the 1930s that has effectively shaped the course of the financial service industry from that time forward.

In the mid-1970s the executive and legislative branches of government became strong proponents of economic deregulation and competition. Congress passed the Securities Amendments Act of 1975 that, among other things, mandated a national securities market with greater access for nonsecurities firms. This act formalized an end to price fixing on securities brokerage, unleashing large declines in institutional brokerage.

The commercial bank sector has also been deregulated. Following the Hunt Commission study Congress enacted the Financial Institutions Act of 1975, which created more competition for commercial banks from thrift institutions by allowing thrifts to offer short-term certificates of deposits and Negotiable Order of Withdrawal (NOW) accounts.

Another major proponent of banking deregulation has been the Federal Reserve and the Comptroller of the Currency, which have supported the entry of commercial banks into related financial areas, such as private placement and acquisition advisory services. It has further allowed commercial banks to greatly increase their assets-to-equity ratio in the last ten years by adding substantial loan assets.

The Depository Deregulation and Monetary Control Act of 1980, and related banking legislation in 1981 and 1982, created additional pressure to promote competition in the banking business. This legislation broadened NOW accounts, making them available nationwide, to all depository institutions. It phases out Regulation Q limits by 1986, thereby fostering interest rate competition between thrift institutions and commercial banks and providing a better return to consumers.* To provide for a more level "playing field" among the depository institutions, it mandated that all depository institutions must maintain minimum non-earning reserve accounts with the Federal Reserve. The 1982 banking legislation permits depository institutions to offer money market liquid asset accounts without interest ceilings; these accounts have grown spectacularly to over $250 billion in the first two months of 1983.

The fuller disclosure of rates of return on the savings function of whole life insurance, urged by the Federal Trade Commission, has caused customers increasingly to switch to term life insurance, which does not generate a future cash value. This trend places a major constraint on traditional asset growth for insurance companies.

This very dismantling of the carefully constructed regulatory patchwork of the financial service industry raises serious questions for the public interest that have not been addressed and clearly remain unanswered as this is written.

These questions revolve around the age-old problem of inherent conflict of interest which has beset the financial service field for centuries. Fifty years ago Congress decided that these conflicts were sufficiently serious to warrant setting up a pattern of regulatory controls and segmentation, many of which have long outlived their usefulness due to economic and technological changes.

What are these changes which have forced this highly regulated and segmented field into new directions? There follows a summary of the major changes that have impacted the financial service industry over the past two decades and particularly since the beginning of the 1980s.

---

*Regulation Q limits the interest that commercial banks and thrifts may pay on passbook and other savings accounts; banking legislation enacted in 1980 schedules a phaseout of these ceilings by 1986.

Competition for the savings of the public has been increasing among sectors of the financial service industry. Concurrent with this competition has been an increase in information on the performance of the various sectors of the industry. Commercial bank trust companies, for example, until the enactment of the Employee Retirement Income Security Act (ERISA) in 1974, operated with a great deal of secrecy. The lack of information on the performance of bank trust companies put the competitors for the highly lucrative pension fund management business at a distinct disadvantage. Coupled with the more open disclosure of investment performance since 1974 has been the revelation that bank trust performance has been uniformly poor in the postwar period (see Table 1.1).

Armed with this information, mutual fund and insurance company representatives have managed to pry considerable amounts of investment management business away from the bank trust companies. Banks once dominated the pension fund management business but have steadily lost market share to their mutual fund and insurance company rivals.

In early 1983, a survey of investment performance, which included stock broker investment adviser results, was published for the first time.[1] This survey revealed that major New York Stock Exchange brokerage adviser units were among the worst per-

TABLE 1.1
Equity Performance: Mutual Funds, Bank-Pooled Funds and Insurance Funds for Various Periods Ending December 31, 1982 (in percent)

	Annual Compound Rate of Return		
	3 Years	5 Years	10 Years
Mutual funds	17.6	19.3	9.4
Bank funds	17.5	16.4	6.7
Insurance funds	17.0	16.1	7.5
Standard & Poor's 500	15.3	14.1	6.6
Consumer Price Index	8.4	9.5	8.7

Source: "Perspective on Mutual Fund Activity," *Investment Company Institute*, Spring 1982, as updated by The Institute.

forming of the 147 advisers included in the survey as shown below in the partial listing:

Selected Major Stock Broker Advisers	Rank (out of 147 Advisers)
Prudential-Bache Securities	143rd
Merrill Lynch	140th
Shearson/American Express	136th
Dean Witter Reynolds Intercapital	91st

If past experience is any guide, this disclosure should have a favorable effect on the future performance of these major firms. There is no place to hide from the glaring publicity of poor performance in the investment management field. This bodes well for the many institutional investors who look to Wall Street for investment management capability.

Deregulation is continuing to free the financial service industry from its regulatory straitjacket. The regulations grew out of the abuses by banks and investment bankers that caused massive conflicts of interest in the financial service industry. During the 1920s investment banking subsidiaries of commercial banks bought securities of companies which had loan relationships with the commercial banking facility. When the deals proved unmarketable the bank sold the securities to their captive trust accounts. Commercial banks had been permitted, under the McFadden Act of 1927, to syndicate public offerings of bond and stock underwritings of the bank for the first time. The dismal record of the bank underwriting affiliates in the late 1920s is said to have contributed to the stock market crash in the early 1930s.

In the 1920s individual corporation boards of directors arranged pools, with the aid of the New York Stock Exchange specialist in each company's stock, to manipulate the price of the corporation's stock on the market. This was justified by a belief that the market did not recognize the true value of the corporation in the trading value of the stock. Corporate managements also enlisted the help of publicists to color and misrepresent the reports of earnings and to play down any bad news that might adversely affect the corporation's stock. In the area of private money management, stock brokers churned investment accounts, ostensibly to improve performance but more often just to create additional trading commissions for the stock broker who managed the accounts.

These abuses were countenanced by a permissive public during the Roaring Twenties, a public lulled into a false sense of security by soaring stock prices that seemed to herald a new era. However, when the stock market collapsed in the early 1930s the public reacted, through Congress, with a series of restrictive legislative acts that split investment banking away from commercial banking, forbade the receipt of brokerage commissions by investment advisors, and required exhaustive registration statements for investment banking underwritings of new securities offerings. The mutual fund industry was severely limited as to the types of investments they could make and the amount of concentration they could maintain in any one industry group. Legislation also restricted stock trading by corporate insiders.

In recent years, with the onset of electronics and the escalating interest rates bred by inflation, financial entrepreneurs have developed new products that successfully bypass the intent of the legislation. Commercial banks and other financial institutions complain that the regulations have outgrown their relevance. They point out that money market mutual funds offer investors all of the advantages of interstate banking through the magic of electronics. They are demanding equal treatment.

As the financial marketplace has expanded, competition has forced a rethinking of age-old ways of doing business, with the goal of reducing costs. Advertising and mass selling have supplanted high cost personal selling in many sectors of the financial service industry. "No-load" mutual funds, that is, funds sold directly to the investor without any commission paid to a broker for securing the sale, now constitute over one-third of fund sales, bypassing the stock broker who used to be the workhorse of the mutual fund distribution system (see Table 1.2). Similarly, advertising has taken on more of the selling job in the stock brokerage field, and the cost of insurance selling is now dominated by low cost direct selling, bypassing the agent with advertising.

Concurrent with the revolution in marketing methods, new products and services are multiplying. Variable interest mortgages

TABLE 1.2
Breakdown of Mutual Fund Sales by Channel of Distribution (billions of dollars)

Source	1972	percent	1982	percent
Broker/dealer	3.3	67	7.9	53
Direct sellers	.8	16	1.5	10
No-load	.8	17	5.5	37
Totals	4.9	100	14.9	100

Source: *1982 Mutual Funds Fact Book,* as updated by the Investment Company Institute, Washington, D.C.

that permit thrift institutions to earn market rates and become viable again accounted for over 50 percent of the new mortgage loans initiated last year. Electronic computer systems deliver more and more of our daily banking and financial needs. Money funds and credit cards, combined into *cash management accounts* by Merrill Lynch and others, have created a new form of deposit/ checking account. In the unregulated overseas market, Merrill Lynch has entered the commercial banking business, and major U.S. money center commercial banks have begun underwriting and trading securities.

Various forms of term and group insurance have eclipsed the once dominant position of whole life coverage. With interest rates reaching double digit levels, deferred annuities with yields of 14 percent or more have been launched and have become far more attractive to the investing public than the old low yield annuities. Income products have received greater promotional emphasis and success than growth products.

In the investment banking field, takeovers to effect mergers and acquisitions have revolutionized corporate financing methods. More mergers and acquisitions were consummated in 1981 than in any previous year on record. The total value of these acquisitions ($82.6 billion) substantially exceeded the capital raised ($63 billion) by syndicated public offerings by traditional investment banking groups.

Thrift institutions, faced with extinction due to disinter- mediation of savings balances and seeking higher returns through money market mutual funds, have developed NOW accounts and six month certificates of deposit to counter this adverse trend. Thrifts received new legislative aid in the fall of 1982 with the passage of new banking legislation permitting them to branch out into commercial and consumer loans in order to reduce their dependence on residential mortgage financing.

"Scrambled merchandising" is growing as financial institutions attempt to diversify into related fields to attract additional investor/depositors.° Banks want to manage and market mutual funds. Brokers are moving into mutual fund money funds, insurance, and deposit banking. Mutual funds want to become banks in order to compete with the new bank liquid asset accounts. Insurance companies want to go into mutual funds and stock brokerage. Reflecting these trends, securities firms have reduced their dependence on stock brokerage commissions to 24 percent of their total revenue in 1982, down from 55 percent in 1973.

Realizing the need to reverse their market share decline from 57 percent of total financial service industry assets in 1946 to an estimated 32 percent of assets in 1982, commercial banks have been mounting an aggressive response. It has begun to work; the industry expanded their geographical presence by adding new offices in major U.S. cities for international and domestic loans. (The McFadden Act restriction on multistate banking does not apply to these offices.)

Commercial banks have begun to move into intermediate-term debt financing of receivables, inventory, and equipment.

Citibank was one of the first to establish a corporate finance department offering private placements, strategic planning, and acquisition analysis. The bank has also sought to add revenues by successfully marketing dividend reinvestment plans with no brokerage charges to corporate shareholders. In the overseas market, Citicorp has become a major securities underwriter for multinational U.S. companies.

°"Scrambled Merchandising" refers to a market strategy that attempts to offer related merchandise to supplement and enlarge the potential volume of a vendor; an example in the field of consumer goods would be to offer shoe polish as a supplemental line in a drug store, or beer and groceries at a rural auto service station.

Most financial services firms have responded to change by trying to compete harder in their own sector of the industry. Casting aside the former understanding that they not call on a competitor's clients, many firms have developed highly organized programs to actively solicit new business.

It is no longer possible to ignore outside threats from new rivals. A principal new competitor of the commercial bank, for example, is the captive finance company. While many finance subsidiaries of manufacturing companies started out to finance the parent company receivables—and still do—many others, such as General Electric Credit, are developing an organizational base and awareness of profit opportunities in related areas such as inventory equipment financing and leasing (see Table 1.3). Because of the nature of their financing, they have tended to concentrate on the smaller industrial companies.

Nonfinancial companies now are entering the financial service field as the appeal of improved returns spreads from the core financial service field into such diverse areas as manufacturing,

TABLE 1.3
The Changing Portfolio Mix of General Electric Credit

Classification of Net Earning Assets at Year-End (in percent)	1970	1980
Consumer		
Direct consumer loans and installment credit	7	15
Appliances, televisions, home furnishings	29	14
Auto leases, recreational vehicles	1	4
Business		
Industrial and commercial loans	24	22
Industrial and commercial leases	8	20
Inventory financing	7	5
Real Estate		
Mobile homes	19	13
Real estate	4	7
Other	1	2

Source: "G.E. Credit: Financial Hybrid," *New York Times,* October 28, 1981, © 1981/82 by The New York Times Company, Reprinted by permission.

retailing, and basic industry. All of these nonfinancial fields seek to diversify into more rapid growth fields as the impact of foreign competition and slowing U.S. industrial growth takes its toll.

Over 60 percent of private U.S. employment is now classified as service-oriented, as compared to about 40 percent service-oriented employment in the immediate postwar period. The Japanese now dominate auto manufacturing which used to account for about 20 percent of the U.S. gross national product when related industries are included. Steel also represents a fast growing sector of the Japanese economy and a major depressed industrial area for the United States. Other nations, for example Germany and Brazil, are significantly increasing their net trade with the United States. Like Great Britain, the United States depends more on its financial and other service industries to improve its balance of payments with the rest of the world. The United States and Great Britain have a comparative trade advantage in the service area because of the advanced state of their electronic technology and the superior educational level of their populations in these new service-oriented fields. British and U.S. banks dominate the financial world just as Toyota and Datsun rule the auto world.

The entrée of nonfinancial enterprises into the world of financial services should trigger a greater level of mass marketing than heretofore. The success of this effort will indicate how much of the mass market representing the lower income segment of the U.S. market can be reoriented toward the financial service industry. Much help has been afforded by recent changes in federal income tax laws. The broadening of the *Individual Retirement Account* (IRA) so that any working person can set aside up to $2,000 per year in a tax-deductible retirement account effectively taps the lower income market for savings, subject to the ability of the average middle-income family to save $2,000 per year, with inflation a constant threat (see Table 1.4). The maximum contribution for self-employed persons (Keogh Plans) was doubled to $15,000 per year as well.

The federal government is again providing help in this regard through renewed efforts to curb inflation and through the three stage basic tax reduction designed to create additional cash income to each family. The question, of course, is whether the middle-income family will spend the tax reductions or save them; only time will tell. Some economists, however, are projecting an annual

TABLE 1.4
The IRA Savings Market
(in billions of dollars)

Savings & loans	15.5
Commercial banks	13.4
Life insurance companies	6.4
Mutual savings banks	5.2
Credit unions	1.6
Mutual funds	5.8
Total IRA funds	47.9

Source: Based on preliminary 1982 esti-mates prepared by the *Investment Company Institute,* December 1982.

increase of $50–60 billion in savings as a result of these new tax incentives.

Mergers in corporate industry spurred by undervalued market values for most U.S. industry, have been growing rapidly over the past 15 years. Some believe the current merger wave exceeds the previous tidal waves of the early part of the century and during the 1920s. Recently, there has been a surge in mergers of financial service businesses for much the same reasons as in the manu-facturing industry (see Table 1.5).

The current market values of financial service businesses are substantially below the replacement value of these franchises. Financial service businesses require people and retail locations, as well as expertise. Thus, insurance companies, banks, credit card companies, and others prefer to buy brokerage companies, mutual funds, and insurance companies rather than embark on the risky and expensive business of starting them from scratch.

The current merger trends of financial service firms reflect a variety of approaches:

- large firms absorbing smaller firms to achieve economies of size and broader service levels
- national firms absorbing regional firms to improve national distri-bution and gain local footholds for investment banking services

TABLE 1.5
Recent Mergers in the Financial Service
Field (in millions)

Acquirer/Acquired	Value of Acquisition
Prudential/Bache	375
Sears/Dean Witter Reynolds	607
Phibro/Salomon Bros.	550
American Express/Shearson	989
Kemper/Bateman, Eichler	60
Kemper/Loewi	64
Shearson/Foster & Marshall	76

Source: Various articles in The New York Times,
Wall Street Journal, Fortune and Forbes.

- disparate mergers involving dissimilar fields, for example, insurance companies absorbing stock brokerages and mutual funds buying up banks
- nonfinancial mergers by retailers/manufacturers seeking new growth opportunities

One tradition which seems to be a casualty of the merger trend is the highly creative star system of the small firm in the securities business. With larger firms, management committees have replaced the individualized managers of old.

For example, the threshold for survival in the mutual fund field has grown to about $5 billion in assets, compared with $2 billion five years ago, and $500 million ten years ago. This increased asset base is required to provide the level of services now considered conventional in this field.

Despite the increase in concentration that these mergers represent, the small speciality house continues to thrive in the financial service field only to change when the managers of these one-service firms opt to expand by broadening their service base.

Almost unnoticed, two formidable competitors have entered into the financial industry: foreign banks and large U.S. corporations.

Foreign banks have seized significant portions of the commercial and industrial loans market. In California, for example, the penetration is already 30 percent. In New York alone, there are more than 210 representative foreign bank offices. Furthermore, foreign banks have purchased several U.S. commercial banks, including Franklin National, Marine Midland, Union Bank, and the New York City branches of Bankers Trust Company. Foreign banks have begun moving in on finance companies, for example, Barclays Bank has acquired American Credit. Foreign banks aggressively seeking corporate business are operating with a distinct competitive advantage. They are not subject to certain reserve requirements of the Federal Reserve, thus giving them a lower cost of capital than their U.S. counterparts. To compete, U.S. commercial banks must reduce their spreads even further or grant more generous terms. In fact, the influence of European pricing has been so strong that U.S. banks have recently been offering companies the choice of a rate based on a spread over U.S. prime or a spread over the London interbank rate. This has exerted even more downward pressure on beleaguered profit margins. Moreover, foreign banks have developed significant positions in several states; U.S. commercial banks generally may not operate branch offices across state lines under the McFadden Act.

Over the long haul, however, commercial banks may feel the greatest pressure from large U.S. industrial companies, once their principal source of revenue. These companies now compete, through their treasury staffs, in the issuance of commercial paper, private placements, acquisition analysis, and pension fund management. Public offerings could even be done in concert with securities firms. It is important to note that the financial services performed by large industrial companies can frequently be accomplished at lower cost and with greater internal control.

Price competition and channel upheavals mark the evolution of the financial service field. "No-load" distribution of mutual fund shares has substantially increased and is gaining on the "load" distribution system based on the broker/dealer. This change results partly from the unwillingness of brokers to sell independent mutual funds, preferring instead to launch their own "house" product and benefit from the reliable fee income that such a move achieves.

Another price change has resulted from the abolishment of fixed stock exchange brokerage commissions in 1975 under a mandate from the Congress. This move has backfired because the benefit of reduced commissions has flowed primarily to the giant institutional investor complexes which control over 50 percent of the stock trading. Small individual investors have seen their commissions increase by about 11 percent while the big institutional investors have benefited from a drop in commissions averaging 68 percent since competitive markets were mandated by Congress. This development indirectly strengthens the sales appeal of money management investing vehicles to the small investor. If a small investor can indirectly gain the economic advantage of a big institution when buying stocks and bonds rather than pay the increased brokerage costs of a small investor, it does not take much convincing to transfer the small investor to mutual funds and away from the "do-it-yourself" investment approach. This is especially true when the mutual fund develops a hard to beat performance record.

Coupled with the freeing up of commission rates, mutual funds have finally convinced the Securities and Exchange Commission (SEC) that they should be allowed to advertise as all other financial service competitors do. Until this change came about, mutual funds were limited to "tombstone" advertising, meaning they could not use selling copy in their ads. It was for this reason that mutual funds were so dependent on the broker/dealer for distribution. Now that mutual funds can advertise almost as freely as Citicorp or Merrill Lynch (however there still remain substantial restrictions), they can compete for the investor's dollar with advertising and the appeal of "no-load" pricing. Despite this easing of restrictions, It will be some time before mutual funds become major advertisers. With one minute of prime time network television costing up to $250,000, mutual fund promotion budgets must choose less expensive and more selective promotional outlets.

Financial markets have become far more volatile, reflecting inflation and international and national uncertainties. The government bond market, which was thought to be a safe place for conservative investors, has now become a trading vehicle. Governments and businesses as a result find it difficult to sell any debt securities, especially those that mature in more than five to ten years. To deal with this reality more and more issuers are innovating, offering zero coupon bonds, convertible issues, silver and gold based (commodity) bonds, variable rate bonds, indexed bonds, and a variety of other financing vehicles. Mutual funds and insurance companies have seized the opportunities of high interest rates to offer money market funds and tax-deferred annuities.

Fiduciary standards, implicit in the separation of the financial service field into different segments are giving way to the need for broader and more diverse packages of services. The marketing concept mandates that the consumer is king and that financial service firms must deliver the services consumers want or run the risk of competitive decline and ultimate bankruptcy. The financial service field is unique however, in that conflicts of interest constantly hamper the investor when he purchases more than one service from a purveyor. For example, if a stock broker manages an investment account for an investor, can the investor be sure that the broker is not churning his account to maximize the broker's commission income rather than the investor's profits? Does a commercial bank impinge on trust account responsibilities when it underwrites a corporate bond or stock issue (as it could in the 1920s) and sells the bond or stock to its controlled accounts? The financial service field is rife with such conflicts. In the consumer goods industry the conflicts that exist are not as damaging to the consumer as those in the financial service field. After all, if a bag of potato chips turns out to be stale, you can probably get your money back from the grocer. Failing that, the consumer is out only 50 cents or so. Compare this with a 50 percent decline in your investment account of over $10,000: can you prove that it was the manager's negligence that accounted for the poor results, especially when everything else is down in price?

These inherent conflicts led Congress in the 1930s to subject the financial service field to its present multilayered system of regulation. The major goal of this action was to segment (or "unbundle") the various services into narrow industry groups, for example, commercial banks for checking accounts and loans, thrift institutions for savings accounts and mortgages, investment banks for underwriting and financing corporations, investment managers for mutual funds, stock brokers for securities transactions, insurance companies for insuring life and property, and so on.

However, the wave of the future, according to consumer surveys, is to "bundle up" these disparate services and afford convenience to the saver/investor. The consumer wants the convenience of a department store when shopping for financial services while demanding the integrity and quality service of a specialty store. Which form will ultimately become conventional only time will tell.

One regulation, the requirement of full publicity, seems to be answering part of the potential abuses implicit in the "bundling" of financial services. Full and complete disclosure of all material information, as embodied in the regulations, has become one of the most effective protections to the investor. This requirement permits financial analysts and the news media to alert investors to unfavorable or favorable trends. Moreover, the very threat of unfavorable publicity acts as a cleansing agent to force financial service suppliers to mind the public interest in their operations. The financial press thus stands as a watchdog for the public, ready to pounce on wrongdoers or underachievers. There is evidence of the validity of this concept. For example, when the notoriously poor performance of bank trust companies in managing the trust accounts and pension funds entrusted to their care was publicized in the financial press, they were forced to step up their efforts. Before ERISA and the disclosures required by the Comptroller of the Currency in the early 1970s, bank trust companies were not required to publish their performance. As a result the banks were not under any pressure to produce superior investment results. With the required publication of their performance records, competitors from mutual funds and insurance companies used comparisons of their own results with those of the banks to take business away from the banks. The banks responded by improving their procedures and thus were able to recapture some of their lost accounts. The consumer ultimately benefited, through improved investment results, from this increase in disclosure and the ensuing competition.

PROBABLE CHANGES IN THE 1980s

The Glass-Steagall Act, which effectively bans commercial banks from investment banking, will probably be repealed. This will, in turn, probably entail the establishment, by banks, of separate investment banking affiliates so that this activity can be differentiated from the deposit/loan activities of the banks, just as the trust division is separated. This separation will tend to prevent basic conflicts of interest from getting out of hand and will provide regulatory agencies with an effective oversight of investment banking activities by the banks.

The repeal of the Glass-Steagall Act will enhance the capital formation ability of industry and help to spur needed investment by U.S. industry in more productive facilities to make American made products and services more competitive in world markets.

Mergers between banks, investment banks, insurance companies, stock brokerages, and mutual funds should continue at an accelerated pace as financial service marketers strive to create "one stop" department stores of finance for the tapping of low- and middle-income families. The congeneric form of financial service so prevalent for centuries in Europe should finally appear in this country.*

In this connection, the ban on interstate bank branching should finally be removed in the 1980s due to the inroads of electronic funds transfer popularized by cash management accounts and money market mutual funds. Increasingly, regional banks will be unable to deliver the sophisticated types of services possible through the miracles of electronic technology. Money center banks will increasingly expand (by merger and in other ways) to offer these services in every nook and cranny of the country.

The distinction between thrift institutions and commercial banks will probably disappear as the highly volatile financial markets force thrifts to become part of the broader financial base of the commercial banks. The thrifts, using their newly legislated lending powers, will adopt commercial and consumer lending as an adjunct to their mortgage loan business. Thrifts have already gained the advantage of checking accounts with their NOW accounts. The variable mortgage loan, which eliminates the financial risk of market rate fluctuation, should become universal in the 1980s. As

---

*"Congeneric" refers to an organization offering products or services of the same general origin, e.g., financial services. It differs from "conglomerate," which refers to organizations offering dissimilar products or services.

noted, 50 percent of the new mortgates last year were variations of the variable rate mortgage.

The consumer should benefit from reduced prices as mass selling in the form of advertising and publicity replace the traditional dependence on high cost personal selling in insurance, mutual funds and stock brokerage.

Foreign banks and financial institutions should further penetrate the U.S. market, providing greater service and increased competition to U.S. firms. Literally hundreds of foreign banks have already opened up offices in the New York and Chicago financial centers. To make U.S. banks more competitive in overseas markets, special banking zones have been created in New York to permit U.S. banks and insurance companies to compete more effectively with foreign concerns. All of this will tend to grow as the current deregulation trend opens up the U.S. market to foreign financial institutions.

The public will recognize the value of allowing financial managers to maintain their investment/savings accounts, continuing a process toward financial intermediation which has its roots (and has advanced further) in the older economies of Western Europe. Although department stores of finance will appear, each will attempt to retain some of the specialty flavor that differentiates and positions each service organization within the financial service field.

NOTE

1. "Brokerage Houses Didn't Fare Well in Survey of 1982 Performance of Investment Advisers," *Wall Street Journal*, Gary Putka, January 10, 1983.

TWO

An Overview of the Financial Service Industry

Although financial institutions have been trying mightily to become diversified department stores of finance, the various institutions continue to retain a specialized flavor that separates them in the mind of the public—a bank is a bank, an insurance company an insurance company. Therefore, it is useful to summarize the various players in the financial service field as they exist today (see Table 2.1).

COMMERCIAL BANKS

The characteristic that distinguishes commercial banks from all other financial service institutions is their ability to take deposits from public and in turn, to loan these monies out to other consumers and business concerns. Commercial banks are the oldest of the financial service group dating back to the 1790 founding of the Bank of New York in New York City by Alexander Hamilton. they are also the largest and most powerful of the financial service group. The primacy of the commercial bank as a depository and lending institution has been challenged by money market funds and the ability of corporations to finance their short term business loans through the commercial paper market.

TABLE 2.1
Growth of U.S. Financial Service Industry (in billions of dollars)

	1946	Percent	1972	Percent	1982*	Percent
Savings & Loans	10.2	4.4	243.6	14.2	714.0	16.1
Mutual Savings Banks	18.7	8.0	100.6	5.8	180.5	4.1
Credit Unions	0.4	0.2	21.7	1.3	83.6	1.9
Life Insurance Cos.	47.5	20.3	231.7	13.5	563.1	12.7
Private Pension Funds	3.2	1.4	152.3	8.9	360.1	8.1
State & Local Retirement Funds	2.9	1.2	71.8	4.2	263.8	5.9
Property Casualty Insurance Cos.	7.1	3.0	64.6	3.8	201.5	4.5
Finance Cos.	4.9	2.1	78.0	4.5	219.1	4.9
Mutual Funds (including Money Market Funds)	1.3	0.6	59.8	3.5	353.4	8.0
Securities Broker/Dealers	3.3	1.4	26.1	1.5	81.0	1.8
Real Estate Investment Trusts	—	—	11.7	0.7	17.7	0.4
Commercial Banks	134.2	57.4	655.0	38,1	1,399.9	31.6
Totals	233.7	100.0	1,716.9	100.0	4,437.7	100.0

*estimated by author.

Source: Board of Governors of Federal Reserve System, *Flow of Funds Accounts*, 1945-82. 1982 totals from 1983 *Prospects for Financial Markets*, Salomon Brothers Inc.

Commercial bank lobbyists are now trying to pressure Congress to allow them to compete in new areas.

Commercial banks have literally hundreds of different services that they offer but they fall into three basic areas.

Deposit Acceptance and Lending—This is by far the largest and most important business activity of banks. Of the $1,399.9 billion in assets currently held by banks, loans and deposits account for more than two-thirds of this total.

Managing Trust and Investment Advisory Accounts—Over half of pension funds are managed by commercial bank trust departments. In addition, personal trusts are dominated by commercial bank trust departments. Trust departments have been receiving considerable competition for accounts in recent years and their dominance has declined. Full disclosure of investment performance has contributed to this erosion. Bank trust departments follow relatively conservative investment policies which have contributed to their lackluster performance. The investment performance standard mandated by ERISA has forced pension fund trustees to seek out the best money managers. Pension funds are a lucrative source of business. Private pension fund industry assets currently total over $400 billion, and this amount is growing at the rate of $15–20 billion in new contributions a year. Mutual fund management companies, insurance companies, investment advisory firms and New York Stock Exchange firms are all competing, at the expense of the commercial banks, for an increased market share of the pension fund management business.

Investment Banking—Although the Glass-Steagall Act of 1933 bans commercial banks from underwriting and distributing securities of private corporations and engaging in the investment business, banks continue their investment banking presence in those areas of investment banking where they are still permitted. For example, commercial banks are important underwriters of state and local securities and engage in widescale merger and acquisition activities, as well as in the private placement of securities of private corporations. Recently, the courts affirmed the right of commercial banks to place privately the commercial paper flotations of their corporate customers. Commercial banks are lobbying for the right to underwrite certain classes of municipal securities that were omitted from the permitted investment banking activities in the Glass-Steagall Act. Specifically, they have lobbied for the right to underwrite revenue bonds. Commercial bank strategy emphasizes small changes in the Glass-Steagall Act, not a sweeping change which Congress would be unwilling to grant all at once. They hope to achieve their ultimate goal of re-entry into all phases of investment banking with step by step changes, eroding the restrictions rather than attempting a head-on attack on Glass-Steagall.

As with thrift institutions, a commercial bank can be state or federally chartered, but since 1980, all commercial banks, along with thrift institutions, must comply with Federal Reserve standards, including maintaining non-earning reserve accounts based on their demand deposit liabilities with the Federal Reserve Bank.

THRIFT INSTITUTIONS

There are three types of thrift institutions: savings and loan associations, by far the largest; mutual savings banks, a hybrid specialty form that thrives in the northeast; and credit unions, the smallest of the thrifts. The breakdown becomes more unclear when it is considered that there are two types of charters, federal and state. The proportion of total assets controlled by state chartered savings and loans is about equal to that chartered under federal regulations. Regulations favor one form or the other depending on the state. The most powerful group of state chartered savings and loans are found in California where much of the housing industry activity has been centered for the past several decades. Mutual savings banks are concentrated in the northeast.

Thrift institutions have been operating under austere conditions in the past decade; the highest interest rates in history have caused massive outflows from individual thrift institutions. Thrifts borrow money short-term and make long-term loans, primarily in the housing mortgage market. Since short-term interest rates have risen to well over 10 percent in recent years, mortgages placed with lower rates caused the thrifts to lose money. Many thrifts have been forced to merge to try to gain a better balance of earning assets.

Regulation Q artificially limits interest paid on passbook savings accounts to 5.25 percent for commercial banks, with thrifts being permitted one-quarter percent more to prevent commercial banks from exacting too great an advantage over the thrifts. Regulation Q was designed to protect the economic viability of thrift institutions. However, in the past decade, with money market rates comfortably above 10 percent, massive outflows have occurred. This disintermediation has caused hundreds of thrifts to cease operations or to be merged into stronger thrift units usually under the auspices of the Federal Home Loan Bank, the federal agency which has primary responsibility for the thrift industry.

The ultimate solution to this problem is for variable rate mortgages to replace the fixed rate mortgages of the past. About 80 percent of savings and loan assets are in mortgages as required by state laws generally. Mutual savings banks are not so restricted and they average about 60 percent in mortgages. The banking legislation enacted in the fall of 1982 by Congress reduces the required investment by savings and loans in mortgages and permits them to make commercial and regular consumer loans with a portion of their assets. Moreover, the federal legislation supercedes any state law or regulation banning "due on sale" clauses in mortgage loans. This will increase the turnover of mortgage loans thus reducing the number of very low rate mortgages outstanding.

Mutual savings banks are the oldest of the thrifts, having grown out of local efforts in eastern seaports to provide safe harbors for seamen's savings and to promote frugality among the nation's seamen. Several of these banks have over $1 billion in assets each.

Credit unions number about 23,000, each representing some affinity group organized on such bases as employment, occupation or residence. Credit unions usually limit their loans to consumer purchases such as automobiles. In recent years, credit unions have been permitted to make loans for housing purchase and home improvement. Credit union growth is limited by the requirement that there be some common bond between members. Credit union assets totaled $83.6 billion in 1982.

INVESTMENT BANKS

Many of the larger investment banks came into being as a result of the divestiture of investment banking units by commercial

banks following passage of the Glass-Steagall Act of 1933. Morgan
Stanley, for example, is the offshoot of the Morgan bank, and First
Boston Corp. grew out of the investment banking departments of
several banks, including First National Bank of Boston. Other
investment banks are affiliates of New York Stock Exchange firms.
For example, Merrill Lynch became a major underwriter by
acquiring White Weld and Co. some years ago. Some others,
however, such as Goldman Sachs and Brown Bros. Harriman, are
pure investment banking firms which date back to the founding of
the nation. Moreover, considerable merger activity has occurred
between investment bankers and nonfinancial companies. For
example, Phibro bought out Salomon Bros. and Bechtel, the
engineering design and construction firm, bought out Dillon,
Read.

Generally, investment banks can be broken down into wholesale houses that rely on other firms to distribute their underwritings
to the public, and retail houses that control their own distribution
through extensive branch office systems nationwide. Merrill Lynch,
Paine Webber and E.F. Hutton would be examples of retail firms
while Goldman Sachs, Morgan Stanley and Lehman Bros. would be
examples of wholesale firms.

The wholesale houses depend on regional as well as national
securities firms to sell their underwritings. This has become a
problem for the wholesale houses because of the merger of regional
firms, seeking a broader service base, into major national firms. For
example, Robinson, Humphrey, a major regional firm located in
Atlanta was recently merged into Shearson/American Express. A
further problem for the wholesale firms is the emergence of the
retail firms as major competitors for investment banking deals.
Wholesale firms, of course, benefit from the lack of a heavy fixed
overhead which characterizes the retail distributing firms. Thus,
with their profits and flexibility in pricing deals they have
advantages over the retail firms. But with the loss of so many
regional firms, the retail firm with its captive distribution consti-
tutes a major threat to the wholesalers.

Investment bankers arrange financing and provide advice for
their clients. Their specialty is in developing unique financing
packages. One veteran of the investment banking world once
described the investment banker as "a tailor who starts with a
button and makes a suit."

Their creativity is the quality that justifies the middleman fee that investment banks charge for their services. A new threat to the entrenched position of the investment bankers was recently posed by the experimental SEC Rule 415 which permits corporations to register large blocks of bonds and stocks for sale at the best market opportunity. This new procedure, called a "shelf registration", effectively bypasses the investment banking fraternity because once a block has been registered, the securities can be sold at any time to one buyer—a pension fund, for example, or an insurance company—directly, on a registered securities exchange, or through the best bid of an investment banker. The major blue chip corporations, traditional investment banking accounts, can now shop their securities offerings around and find the best deal. It is thought that small firms will continue to seek out the services of investment bankers because their securities do not have the national ranking thought necessary for direct sale. Since this experimental rule was promulgated by the SEC early in 1982, some $18 billion in securities offerings have been transacted using the shelf registration procedure.

A cross-section of the many financing aids afforded by investment bankers follows.

Venture Capital Activities—Most investment banking relationships grow out of an early private financing of a company when it is in the development stage. Investment banks establish a relationship early, with young, emerging enterprises. Recently, several investment firms have financed venture capital partnerships as affiliates to the investment banking house. This trend should gain impetus from the competitive reality of shelf registrations and the accompanying loss of some of the large Fortune 500-type industrial clients.

Underwritings—The investment banker buys blocks of securities for resale through banking syndicates organized by the investment bankers. This is the traditional vehicle for corporate financing. Some $76 billion in new capital was raised for corporations through such public offerings in 1982.

Private Placements—The investment banker, as agent, arranges the private sale to institutional investors rather than through an underwriting. This route is usually taken for smaller companies whose securities are not suitable for public distribution. The private placement market has suffered in recent years because of cash flow problems of life insurance companies, the major buyers of private placements. Life insurance companies have suffered from disinter-mediation brought about by the decline in the sale of whole life insurance policies and the increase in policy loans of cash values at low interest rates as specified in individual policies. Policy holders borrow money typically at five percent and reinvest it in the money market at interest rates considerably in excess of these costs. Private placements totaled $22 billion in 1982.

Mergers and Acquisitions—This has been the most important area of investment banking in recent years as corporations find that it is cheaper to buy an existing business than it is to start one from scratch. The expertise of investment bankers is particularly impor-tant in designing a merger or takeover proposal. Mergers and acquisitions in 1981 were at record levels, exceeding $80 billion, but are estimated to have fallen back to $54 billion in 1982.

Financial Advisory—This is the continuing service through which traditional investment banking ties are maintained. Normally a lead banker will sit on the client's board of directors and will receive monthly financial statements. This close, ongoing relationship grew out of the requirement that an investment banker exercise due diligence in conducting investment banking activities.

MUTUAL FUNDS

The youngest of the financial service firms, having been launched in the late 1920s, mutual funds had their greatest growth in the 1960s during the great bull market in equities that occurred in that decade, and more recently in the 1970s with the intro-duction of money market mutual funds (see Table 2.2). Money funds now comprise $209 billion in assets, more than four times the size of common stock fund assets which have been the core business of the mutual funds since the 1920s.

Mutual funds have older brethren in the form of the closed-end trusts that were formed in the heady days of the stock market

TABLE 2.2
Assets of Mutual Funds
(in billions of dollars)

Type	1972	1982
Aggressive growth	3.5	9.6
Growth	20.2	19.0
Growth & income	24.9	22.0
Balanced	7.3	3.1
Income	3.9	5.9
Bond	NA	9.1
Municipal bond	NA	7.4
Option income	NA	0.8
Money market	NA	209.0
Total assets	$59.8	$285.9

NA-not available.

Source: 1982 Mutual Fund Fact Book, as updated by the *Investment Company Institute*, Washington, D.C.

speculation in the 1920s. The closed-end funds do not redeem shares of shareholders as is the case with mutual funds. A shareholder must sell his closed-end shares on the New York Stock Exchange or the over-the-counter market, if not listed on the exchange, and the price that he receives frequently is at a discount to the book value of his underlying investment (net asset value).

Equity funds, the original backbone of the mutual fund industry, experienced net redemptions in the 1970s as investors reacted negatively to the underperformance of equity funds during that period. More recently, in the 1980s, equity funds have had a revival of popularity as performance of the high technology and emerging growth mutual funds have caught the attention of investors. During the 1970s, money market mutual funds and bond funds were the more popular types of vehicle and the sales of these income-oriented products dominated the marketing experience. In 1982, another trend became evident. Dreyfus Corp., a major mutual fund manager, made application to, and received approval from, the appropriate banking authorities to acquire control of a commercial bank.

LIFE INSURANCE COMPANIES

Life insurance is an ancient industry. The original company came into being about the same time as the birth of our nation in the late 1700s. The industry has experienced considerable turbulence in recent years. Whole life insurance once the bulwark of industry sales, has declined in market share while term, group, and other noncash value policies have gained (see Table 2.3). The yield on whole life insurance cash values averages only 4 to 5 percent per year and the average policy holder has followed the old adage of "buy term and invest the rest" in higher yielding money market investments.

Although the life insurance industry has been around for over 200 years, the bulk of its growth has been since the early part of this century. Up to that point the life insurance industry frequently was characterized by sharp dealing by fringe operators who exploited the fine print in the policies. Socially detrimental hybrid products, such as "tontines" led to widescale state investigations, notably the Armstrong Commission in New York. The effect of these investigations was to create a web of state regulation that continues to be the primary regulator of the insurance industry. With the McCarran-Ferguson Act of 1945, Congress recognized that the public interest was best served by the continued regulation of the insurance industry by the individual states. Thus, the insurance

TABLE 2.3
Life Insurance by Type
(in billions of dollars)

Type	1975	1980
Whole life	100.8	167.0
Term	91.7	228.0
Group	94.6	102.0
Credit	49.0	175.0
	$336.1	$672.0

Source: Best's Review, Vol. 81, No. 9, January 1981, p. 12, A. M. Best Co.

industry is the only sector of the financial service field that does not have a substantial layer of federal regulation.

Another anomaly of regulation is the situation existing in New York State. New York State insurance regulations specify that in order for any life insurance company to do business in that state, it must comply with New York State regulations, which are unusually restrictive. As New York State is a particularly lucrative market for life insurance, the effect of this regulation is to force all companies to conform. The regulations limit investments by life insurance companies to 10 percent of assets and limit agent commissions to 55 percent of the first year premium and 15 percent thereafter on whole life business and 15 percent of premium on all term insurance. Elsewhere, insurance companies can pay their agents as much as 140 percent of the first year premium on whole life policies. Because of these restrictions, many national companies have set up separate companies (affiliates) to operate in New York and thereby circumvent the restrictive nature of New York state regulations elsewhere.

Due to the declining popularity of whole life insurance, a number of new life insurance products have been launched to try to bolster cash value life sales. The most successful of these products is Universal Life. This product provides for the segregation of the policyholder's cash values into a separate account in order to increase the yields. As a result of this segregation, Universal Life has been able to offer returns on cash values approaching 14 percent. Some believe that Universal Life will become the primary insurance product in a few years. Variable life insurance is another product designed to offset inflation's erosion of policy values. Here the insurance company guarantees to pay a death benefit which adjusts for the inflation that has occurred during the term of the insurance. Another life insurance product is the sale of deferred annuities contracts. With yields in fixed income securities at or near all-time highs, life insurance companies have increased sales of deferred annuities funded with high yield investments. Since the income on these investments is tax-deferred as long as the income stays in the annuity company, sales of this product have increased substantially in recent years. The deferred annuity contract was used with considerable success until the Internal Revenue Service ruled that the tax shelter was invalid when the deferred annuity contract was funded with mutual fund shares. The IRS ruled that unless the annuity investment was exclusively for the benefit of the deferred annuity contract holder it did not qualify as an insurance asset. As a result of this ruling, insurance companies have altered their insurance contracts so the funding for deferred annuity contracts is a product exclusively for the deferred annuity company and not to be sold to the general public except as part of the deferred annuity program. In 1982 Congress passed legislation clarifying the tax treatment of deferred annuity contracts.

PROPERTY AND CASUALTY COMPANIES

Property and casualty insurance differs considerably from life insurance in that losses due to calamity are less predictable than death claims under life insurance. Consequently, underwriting results for casualty companies are cyclical. In recent years, due to inflation and crime, underwriting results have been quite poor. This has led to frequent premium increases to offset these losses.

Casualty insurance differs from life insurance in the marketing of the product. Life insurance, being optional, must be "sold", whereas property insurance is essential, especially in home and automobile ownership. Thus the marketing of life insurance usually depends greatly on the individual insurance agent, whereas the consumer will shop carefully to obtain the best and lowest cost coverage when purchasing casualty insurance. For this reason, most property and casualty insurance is sold by direct writers or by insurance brokers who place their business with the company offering the lowest cost coverage for their clients.

NEW YORK STOCK EXCHANGE FIRMS

The earliest form of stock brokerage was incorporated in 1792 under the terms of the New York Stock and Exchange Board, the predecessor of the New York Stock Exchange. Stock brokerage is a cyclical business and most firms have diversified into other financial service fields such as money management, investment banking, money market mutual funds and other mutual funds, real estate brokerage, and other related lines. Mergers of regional firms into large national firms and large national firms into other financial service complexes have changed the industry from small to giant units in the past 20 years.

In addition to the unpredictability of stock trading volume and prices, since May 1975 stock brokers have had to compete in price as well. Fixed stock commissions were written into the original constitution of the New York Stock Exchange in 1792, but in 1975 the SEC under a Congressional mandate ruled that stock brokers from that time forward must compete in price. This move has resulted in drastic price reductions for institutional investors and corresponding price increases for individual investors.

NONFINANCIAL COMPANIES

A potpourri of nonfinancial companies, eyeing the rapid growth of financial services and possessing the computer and other business strengths to compete in the financial service arena, are enlarging their role in this area. Retailing firms such as Sears have entered the field by acquiring large existing financial service firms. Credit card companies such as American Express have acquired large New York Stock Exchange firms. These firms seek to build on their existing credit card systems and enter the expanding world of money funds, investment banking, and cash management services. It is likely that as consumers expand their savings programs in IRAs and Keogh plans, activity by nonfinancial firms will also expand. The nonfinancial retailing firms have recognized expertise in tapping low- and middle-income markets.

A potential legal stumbling block might force nonfinancial companies to divest their new financial service subsidiaries in much the same way as the Glass-Steagall Act of 1933 forced the split-up of commercial banking and investment banking. William Isaac, head of the Federal Deposit Insurance Corp., warned nonfinancial companies in early 1983 that new rules under study would force divestiture of financial service companies by retailers and other businesses not previously affiliated with finance. Stating that the Federal Reserve supported his position, Mr. Isaac stressed that "there are enormous problems, potential conflicts, when . . .

intermingling banking and general commerce." Mr. Isaac also questioned mergers of brokerage firms with banks and credit card companies. It was not immediately clear if the changes sought would require Congressional legislation.[1]

---

1. "Financial Services Get New Scrutiny," *The New York Times*, January 28, 1983.

THREE

The Marketing Concept: Adaptation to the Financial Service Field and Conflict with the Fiduciary Standard

At the center of the controversy over regulation is the need for the financial service field to adapt to modern marketing theory; that is the marketer must discover the needs and desires of the consumer and shape his product service to both satisfy the consumer and make a profit.

However, the financial service field embodies substantial conflicts of interest between the profit interests of the purveyors of these services and the desire to blend together many services under an umbrella, or one stop department store of finance.

The conflicts are vivid in the stock brokerage field. The traditional broker (or "stock jockey") is going the way of the stock ticker. A new "customer's man" is evolving who offers a dizzying variety of financial services that were once the province of lawyers, tax men, and accountants. With brokers exercising cradle-to-grave control over family finances, some questions arise. Can the broker maintain the degree of impartiality of the lawyer/tax adviser given his vested interest in the commissions generated? Will present safeguards be sufficient to prevent abuses of trust? Brokers now market insurance tax shelters, real estate, mutual funds (including money market funds), home relocation services, financial planning, loan resales, commodities futures, and oil exploration partnerships, as well as stocks and bonds. Brokers sell some products more than others because commissions are higher. Merrill Lynch tried to address this problem by paying brokers a salary and bonuses, rather than having them rely on straight commissions.

Another problem area involves churning investor accounts. When stock brokers manage an investment account for a client with full discretion to buy and sell securities, there is an economic incentive to turnover the assets in the account in order to generate stock brokerage commissions. Thus, the broker's goals are potentially in conflict with the client's interests.

To cope with this inherent conflict of interest, the securities regulators have instituted strict rules to protect the interests of the investor.

Another conflict revolves around the practice of a broker receiving a management fee for managing an investor's account and at the same time receiving stock brokerage commissions on securities transactions in the client's account. Congress felt it was unsound for a broker to receive dual compensation and passed legislation to ban stock brokers from executing stock brokerage orders for those accounts for which they would receive a fee for managing assets. It was felt the client's interest was better served by separating stock executions from investment management.

What happens to the brokerage order now that the broker can not execute it? It is given to another nonaligned broker who executes the order and receives the commission. But conflict of interest again rears its ugly head. If a broker receives substantial stock brokerage commissions from a managing asset broker, he may provide services to that managing asset broker in recognition of the profitability of the portfolio executions. The stock broker will perhaps offer research assistance, or lucrative underwriting positions in "hot deals", or free trips to the Bahamas. This procedure, called reciprocal business, has been at the core of the SEC's concern for investor interests over the past 20 years. The solution in this case was multifaceted. In addition to the commission ban on managing asset brokers the SEC mandated that the New York Stock Exchange eliminate fixed stock commissions. This action served to promote competition and lower stock brokers' fees (see Table 3.1). By driving fees down, the SEC felt that reciprocal practices would lose their appeal because the excess profit has been squeezed out of the brokerage rate by competition. If this seems bizarre, it is, but

TABLE 3.1
Brokerage Commissions After "May Day"*

| | Effective Commission Rates | | | |
| | Small Individual Investors | | Large Institutional Investors | |
	Cents per Share	As a Percent of Principal	Cents per Share	As a Percent of Principal
1975 (May Day)	50.1	2.03	15.0	0.57
1975	50.0	2.09	10.9	0.40
1976	50.4	2.02	10.3	0.33
1977	49.8	2.10	8.9	0.30
1978	53.0	2.11	8.2	0.31
1979	54.9	2.08	7.9	0.28
1980	59.3	1.91	7.5	0.25
1981	55.5	2.25	5.5	0.26

*May Day: refers to the day (May 1) that stock commissions became negotiable in 1975.

Source:"Commission Rate Trends 1975–1981,"Securities and Exchange Commission, July 7, 1982.

how else can the regulators act to protect the interest of the public investor who wants top flight money management when he goes to Wall Street for help?

However, there is a negative aspect to all this. Before the introduction of negotiated competitive commissions, all investors paid roughly the same rate. It is true that the big investors were given volume discounts to reflect the economics of big block trades (it costs the same amount for a broker to executive a 10,000 share order as for a 100 share order), but even the volume discounts left enough potential profit so that reciprocal business deals continued to thrive in one form or another. It has been rumored, but denied by the banks, that new bank headquarters office buildings were tenanted by stock brokers who looked to the bank landlords for stock brokerage business to offset the high rents necessary to make the new building venture viable. Where did the stock brokerage business come from? From the bank's captive trust advisory accounts which are managed on a fully discretionary basis. Thus stock brokerage was given to brokers to help pay the rent, not to help the bank manage the trust accounts better. If true, it explains why bank investment performance has been scandalously poor over the years.

The pity is that the move to competitive commissions that took the fat out of institutional brokerage commissions did not work to the benefit of the small investor who now pays more than ten times the commission rates paid by giant institutional investors. The small investor does not have the clout to negotiate a lower commission with the giant brokerage firms. Besides, someone has to pay for the lower commissions brokers now receive from their institutional customers. After the unfreezing of commission rates, brokers increased commissions on small trades to compensate for the deep competitive cuts they were forced to make in commissions on big trades to the affluent investors and institutions who now shop around for the best rates. Thus, the 300 or so giant buyers receive stock brokerage services for an average cost of 5 to 10 cents a share versus 55 cents a share for the small buyer. The department store route or some other mass buyer route, for example, mutual funds, better serves the investor in terms of reducing transaction costs.

Other Examples of Real and Potential Conflicts of Interest

Conflicts of interest are not restricted to stock brokerage transactions and money management. The financial service field abounds in such conflicts.

The corporate financing field of investment banking is rife with potential conflicts. One abuse involves the misuse of inside information. A classic case of such misuse was revealed last year by the blue ribbon investment banking firm of Morgan Stanley, in its highly profitable mergers and acquisition department. Several young, bright, and socially well-placed associates of the firm relayed secret information about pending mergers, enabling the recipients of the information to profit in the stock market. Typically merger strategy involves use of tender offers for two or three times the going price of the target's company's common stock. Insiders parlayed this secret information into stock profits, in violation of laws that forbid trading on inside information. The leak occurred despite strict internal controls at Morgan Stanley to prevent such "tipping." Wall Street and the business community was shocked by these revelations. Internal security in the major firms was tightened to prevent any recurrence of the problem.

Another example of the potential for abuse and conflict of interest is in the sale of life insurance. An insurance agent can sell a customer term insurance at a significantly lower premium cost than for whole life insurance. Then the client can invest the premium savings in higher yielding money market funds. The difference between the commissions earned on term life sales versus whole life creates the conflict. Typically, the agent receives a 15 percent commission on term insurance policies while he receives a first year commission of 55 percent of the annual premium (in New York— up to 140 percent elsewhere) on whole life insurance policies. Thereafter, second and later year commissions on whole life policies scale down to 15 percent as in term insurance. Obviously life insurance companies like to sell whole life because the premiums are scaled at a fixed level to reflect the life insurance risk over the average life of the covered individual. This, in turn, means that whole life premiums run many times higher than term premiums during the early years of an insured individual. The life insurance companies invest those excess cash values from whole life premiums in a relatively low yield composite portfolio representing the companies' policy reserves and they provide the policy holder with a very low rate of return. Typically, the earnings of policyholders on their paid up cash values, that is, the excess that accrues each year because of whole life premium pricing methods, averages only 4 to 5 percent. The market place is correcting this conflict however, by providing new forms of insurance coverage in the form of Universal Life, increased sale of term and group policies, and investment of the difference between term premiums and whole life premiums in high yielding safe money market funds. Moreover, state insurance regulators are very tough with insurance agents who "scalp" unsuspecting clients in the sale of whole life.[*] They can lose their licenses and thereby, their livelihood.

---

[*]"Scalping" refers to the practice of turning over insurance coverage solely to generate extra sales commissions for the sales representative.

Conflicts arise from the differing motives of the loan and trust departments in a bank. The loan department might try to pressure the trust department to avoid selling out the securities of a commercial loan customer from the bank-managed trust accounts. This conflict has caused commercial banks to separate their trust departments into separate affiliates so that loan departments can not have influence over or knowledge of the trust department's investment portfolio.

Another flagrant conflict of the past was between the trust departments and the investment banking affiliates of commercial banks. If an underwriting by the investment banking affiliate was going badly, the trust department frequently would buy up the remaining unpurchased shares. This often resulted in losses to the trust accounts and in 1933 Congress passed the Glass-Steagall Act which banned commercial banks from engaging in most investment banking and securities activities. The commercial bank lobby is pushing aggressively to repeal portions of the original Glass-Steagall Act that forbid them from underwriting municipal revenue bonds. Their justification is that the Glass-Steagall Act specifically permitted commercial banks to underwrite municipal general obligation bonds. Commercial banks claim that Congress would have included revenue bonds if they had existed in volume in the early 1930s. Municipal revenue bonds have only become popular in the past decade as a way of gaining voter approval for new municipal spending programs requiring funding. Commercial banks claim the omission of revenue bonds from the 1933 Act was an oversight which Congress should correct. Bankers assert that the ban on commercial bank participation in municipal revenue bond financing endangers the ability of urban areas to finance their renaissance.

REGULATORY TRENDS

The financial service field, because of inherent conflicts, is probably the most regulated of any industry in the United States, excepting public utilities which owe their regulation to their monopoly status. The past two presidents, a Democrat and a Republican, have come out strongly for deregulation of industry in hopes that competition will prove a better regulator of economic activity than government. Most of the regulations grew out of the early abuses alluded to previously. Proponents of deregulation state that full disclosure is a more powerful force than regulation for preventing the abuses stemming from conflicts of interest. Ten years ago the office of the Comptroller of the Currency, which shares jurisdiction over the nation's commercial banks with the Federal Reserve, and the banking commissioners of each state mandated that bank trust companies must publish the average performance of the trust accounts managed by the bank. This public disclosure works in favor of the customers because the bank does not want to see poor investment performance published for the public to view. Such poor performance damages the image of the bank and hastens the withdrawals of trust management business to competitors. The bank is forced, by the revealing light of publicity, to tighten up and improve its investment procedures.

Banks, in their efforts to repeal portions of the Glass-Steagall Act, have contended that over the past 50 years, while they have been restricted to essentially the deposit and loan business and trust accounts, they have learned to operate their businesses with the public interest paramount and they will be statesmanlike in their approach to potential conflicts.

Contrary to this industry-wide push for deregulation is the position of the Securities and Exchange Commission. The SEC believes that the conflicts inherent in the securities business are so fundamental that the only solution is for further segmentation, e.g., "unbundling." The SEC promotes further "unbundling" of different services identified and restricted to specialty vendors who offer specific services and charge for each separately. For example, stock executions, in the SEC view, involve transactions, investment advice, custody, margin loans, and other specific services. The SEC would like to see brokers either charge separately for each of these services or divest themselves of all but a limited number. This extreme viewpoint will not prevail as it is essentially unworkable and ignores the wave of deregulation and competition that is working its way through the regulatory agencies of the federal government.

Nowhere in the financial service field do the regulations stifle competition as much as in the commercial banking field. All states, and later the federal government, passed prohibitions against interstate banking. The McFadden Act of 1927 forbade federally chartered commercial banks from branching privileges greater than those in the states in which they operated. The Douglass amendment extended this ban to bank holding companies. These laws were designed to protect the small depositor from the evils of Wall Street and to protect the small home town bank from being swallowed up by the big money center banks.

The effect of all this is an inefficient patchwork quilt system of banks. The British system, by contrast, contains four money center banks with an international branch system of about 3,000 branch units each. A United Kingdom resident can transfer money and transact banking business with ease through his bank's far flung domestic and overseas branches.

In contrast, the United States unit banking system has thousands of individual banks and depositors must rely on an antiquated and inefficient correspondent banking system. If the U.S. system permitted interstate branching, the large money center banks would absorb regional and local units and offer a wider horizon to banking customers. Possibly 20 giant systems would evolve (roughly equivalent to the British system adjusted for relative population) which could lead to 60,000 banking offices— about four times the number of retail banking offices under the present restricted banking system.

In the absence of interstate branching, computer technology has found ways to streamline service to bank customers. Since credit card companies can transact business over state lines (they are not defined as banks) much of the interstate banking business has been taken over by nonbank credit card systems. More recently, money funds of the mutual funds, offering the ease of wire transfer, high yields, and checking account privileges, have created "near bank" interest-bearing checking accounts.

Thus commercial banks are barred from competition because of the antiquated theories of the need to protect small banks and local communities from the perils of the money center banks. The effect of the regulation is to restrain trade and deny to the consumer the benefits of service and convenience. Moreover, the effect of these restrictive regulations has been to force the financial service industry to find loopholes in the regulation in order to provide the services demanded by the public. This has been accomplished by combining the credit card, checking account, and money fund into the cash management account.

Adapting to the Marketing Concept

Now we come to an examination of the necessity for financial services to adapt to modern marketing theory. Peter Drucker, one of the brilliant marketing minds of our age observed that "marketing is so basic that it cannot be considered a separate function . . . . It is the whole business seen from the point of view of its final result, that is, from the customer's point of view."[1]

The professional marketer continuously studies consumer needs and wants, develops products to satisfy those needs and wants, tests product validity, prices products, establishes distribution channels, communicates with the public, monitors customer attitudes, and revises marketing plans to reflect consumer concerns and finally earns a profit.

This approach involves three basic steps: market segmentation for planning purposes, analysis of specific market segments, and evaluation or segment "sorting." Following these steps gives a clear picture of exactly how a firm looks in the marketplace *vis-à*-vis customers and competition. What is more important, it provides a sound basis for allocating marketing resources for maximum results. Unfortunately market research has been limited in the financial service arena and it is not clear whether the public prefers to buy their financial services in a "department store" or a "specialty store."

To many in the financial field maximization of resources means creating department stores of finance to serve the needs of the public with particular emphasis on the mass market. Wall Street works fine for the high-income market and for institutions. Wall Street pursues this upper income crust aggressively. The carriage trade will never need to go to Sears to buy stocks and insurance. But if a financial service provider wants to tap the lower income market, it must do as Henry Ford did with the automobile. It must design a low cost, "no-frills" package that can be sold for a very attractive price but that yields a profit and offers an unbeatable value to the small investor. Sears and some of the other retailing and consumer goods giants feel that consumers will prefer, in the long run, the economy and convenience of the supermarket or department store to the increased costs of the specialty store. Mass and specialty systems may co-exist as the financial service businesses of the future. The supermarket will serve the low- and middle-income investor interested in only minimal service—a mutual fund, insurance, or an IRA or Keogh plan. Upper-income investors and institutions will continue to do business with the specialty boutiques which provide service in return for commissions and fees from the large investor.

Some raise the question whether "bundling" many services into packages available through a mass distribution system will lower quality of service delivered. Will packaging a variety of service skills, for example, insurance, banking, stock brokerage, investment management, credit cards, and loans lead to a dilution of the quality of each service offered, or can the packages maintain the service level to the satisfaction of the investor?

The competitive market guarantees that, if quality suffers under the "bundled" or "umbrella" approach, the specialty vendor will gain at the expense of the mass merchandiser. Further, the requirement of full and open disclosure ensures that competition will have beneficial results.

In summary, regulations grew out of early abuses. Full disclosure and competition seem to correct these abuses and conflicts. Regulations tend to limit competition and create narrow fiefdoms that (while preventing conflicts of interest) flaunt the principle of the marketing concept, which postulates that the consumer is king and his preference must become the law of the markets. This law seems to say that consumers, particularly smaller investors, prefer mass merchandising supermarket approaches because they provide a level of service generally unavailable to the small investor. Higher income investors and institutions, on the other hand prefer the privacy and service of the specialty vendor. Thus the picture of markets that is emerging reflects diversity, change, and substantial growth.

NOTE

1. "How to find out what business your bank is in," *Bank Marketing*, November 1979.

FOUR

Market Research and New Product Development in the Financial Service Field

The financial services field is about where consumer products companies were in 1945 in relation to market research and new product development. Very few financial service organizations have on-going market research divisions. This is particularly true in the securities industry. Most new products are not pretested but launched and, if successful, expanded and aggressively promoted.

Most of the marketing efforts made are targeted at the high-income market where market demographics are considered sufficiently attractive to permit some market research to determine the preferences of the high-income consumer for new financial services. As the financial service field broadens its offerings to the mass- and middle-income savings market all of this will, of course, need to change. Mass merchandising will be critical in structuring economically feasible services for these consumers of modest means. Customer perceptions and opinions will determine the shape of the service and the delivery system for making the service available to the small investor/saver. This will in turn determine the success of one brand versus another. Success will depend not only on the quality of the service offered but on whether the brand focuses on a sufficiently large segment of the market perceived to have needs/wants for the particular attribute or benefit offered by each service. Thus consumer and investor research will have to

43

increase substantially to achieve mass merchandising and market segmentation.

The entrée of the nonfinancial companies, like Sears and other mass merchandisers, into the financial service field should spur new product and market research. These companies will seek to apply the lessons learned in consumer product marketing to similar marketing challenges in the financial service field.

New product development in the financial service field has one key advantage over tangible consumer product development. To offer a new financial service no new physical plant is needed, just the development of the computer software to implement the new service and some marketing material. Thus failures in the financial service field do not result in the multimillion dollar losses common to the consumer product field.

Stocking the distribution channels does not pose the same problems as in the consumer package goods industry. There are no packages to stock, just the intangible service offered by a new computer-based program. Thus the offering circular or brochure typically embodies all of the information that is printed on the package in the consumer service field.

In the financial service field most retail outlets are controlled by the vendor, facilitating the introduction of new services. Stock brokers have their own branch offices, banks their own bank branches and, increasingly, mutual funds are relying on direct selling through newspaper and radio advertising on a "no-load" basis. Inevitably, this trend is leading to the opening of satellite offices by the mutual fund entrepreneurs.

The major drawback to new product development in the financial service field is the virtual absence of patent protection. To qualify for a patent, an inventor/developer must design an invention which was not known or used before in the United States. As a rule patents are difficult to obtain in the service industry and in the application of computer science. Although about 60 percent of all patent applications result in patents for the applicants, very few service/computer-based patent applications have been approved. The patent office has ruled in these cases that computer hardware inventions are generally patentable but software design does not represent a novel and new discovery but merely a reworking of existing knowledge. Merrill Lynch has received a patent for its cash management service which has been challenged in court by Paine Webber, a major competitor. Merrill Lynch's application for patent protection identified 162 steps in the processing of its service as "unique and novel" and therefore worthy of patent protection. Apparently the U.S. Patent and Trademark Office agreed. Paine Webber, in its lawsuit in federal court said that Merrill Lynch, the nation's largest brokerage house, had claimed that Paine Webber's Resource Management Account usurped Merrill Lynch's patent rights for its Cash Management Account. The outcome of the court case challenging Merrill Lynch's patent right will have great implication for the future of new product development and marketing in the financial service field.

Prior to the Merrill Lynch patent award, financial service strategists had believed they could legally adopt a competitor's new service. In turn they knew that any marketing edge a new product or service gave their company was only temporary. In a few months or a year their more responsive competitors would have their own version available. There is a gap between having the legal right to copy a competitor's product and being able to do so on a timely basis. The infrastructure of existing computer hardware and software, people, resources, organization, and procedures takes time and money to change. Time means loss of profit, market share, and momentum to a competitor with the better product and service already in place. Whatever the outcome of the Paine Webber court challenge, the Merrill Lynch cash management service has already signed on 900,000 customers with total assets in excess of $50 billion, dwarfing their competitors in this segment of the market. New product planning thus tries to forecast trends two to three years in advance to assure the availability of new products when needed.

While it is true that new service products have always been plentiful, most of them have proven to be transitory. Traditional standby products have maintained their majority share of annual sales. Whole life insurance, despite its disadvantages in failing to provide adequate returns on the policy holders cash values, continues to provide a 25 percent share of the total new market for life insurance coverage.

Another problem in introducing new products is the struggle to gain the acceptance of both the field sales force and the clients of the financial service firm. Chase Manhattan Bank has for example, been unable to promote successfully its "pay bills by telephone" service because of a lack of support at the retail level and a consumer lethargy to get involved in this new convenience. Sales personnel invariably are hesitant to abandon older services that have proved successful in meeting their needs and those of their clients. Much testing, learning and comparisons are needed to convert the "doubting Thomases."

Regulatory constraints further delay introduction of new services. In the life insurance business, for example, discussion with several state insurance departments is required to get approval on policy provisions, reserves, and cash values. Important tax consequences may need discussion with federal and state tax authorities. Indeed, the originating company may have to mount intensive efforts to get changes in laws, regulations, or private letter rulings. Current factors impeding new service introduction include inflation, consumerism, and new regulations.

The erratic decade of the 1980s is here and we have little alternative but to accept the upheavals that are implicit in a period of rapid change. Marketing strategists will be forced to develop action plans that reflect uncertainty rather than try to eliminate it. While there may be safely isolated niches in the market place, only a handful of the financial service companies will be able to "hide" from the marketplace in so-called "safe harbors." The bulk of the industry will have to deal with the reality of the 1980s by accident or skill.

Market planning and research involves several key steps. The first and most difficult step is to convince top management of the need for action in the midst of uncertainty. The traditional success of the "watch-wait-wade-widen" strategy will not work in the atmosphere of dynamic change lying ahead, especially if patent rights become widely available for new financial service product areas.

Steps to Take in New Product Planning In the Life Insurance Field

1) Identify the company's key measures of success. What are the strengths and weaknesses of the company?
2) Establish a competitive monitoring system to determine what other

companies are doing, including feedback from agents and field supervisors.

3) Examine the computer and manual systems for their flexibility. It may be that the first step in the process is to replace old machines with more flexible systems so that adaptation to competitive moves can be more rapid and timely.

4) Gear up the actuarial staff to become more efficient in making the necessary changes. They should review their computer systems and "bone up" on state regulations.

5) Establish a "top-down" attitude about the importance of responsiveness to product changes. Clarify the marketing philosophy of the company, including its pricing philosophy.

6) Conduct fact finding sessions within the company to determine costs and requirements to implement significant product change. What costs are involved in changing markets, marketing style, and services? What actions need to be taken with existing agents or policies as a result of product change?

7) Install a management change system to react quickly to sudden competitive changes in new products offered.[1]

In structuring a new service product program, a key advantage most financial service firms have is control over retail outlets. With this advantage financial service marketing executives can offer their new service in a limited number of outlets to test its reception by both the public and the sales force. This can be arranged with a minimum of delay and in total secrecy, until such time as it is deemed important to publicize the new service.

The financial press has a voracious appetite for new service ideas and the initial promotion of a new service usually relies heavily on publicity engendered by press agents in the employ of the financial service organization.

Much of the market research available has been conducted by the trade associations of various financial services. The following summarizes the research that has been published so far.

A PROFILE OF THE TYPICAL INVESTOR/SAVER

Studies show that the average individual is conservative and opposed to taking risks. Of course, every time the stock market goes on a speculative spree, many investors abandon their innate conservativeness and plunge into the stock market to make a killing—unfortunately often to find losses instead of gains. But this is the extreme of individual behavior. Usually the average investor is extremely cautious. The great success of money market funds stems directly from this conservative bent.

Investors like service and have so far shunned "unbundled" services, preferring to do all of their business under one roof in a specific area of the financial services, for example, in stock brokerage transactions. Higher income individuals prefer doing business with specialty shops on the theory that they get more for their money by dealing with specialists rather than with generalists.

Despite considerations of convenience the investor distrusts large financial complexes, preferring small units out of fear of losing out in a large context. Thus the investor believes that the boundaries separating the various financial services are desirable even though there are advantages to packaging all of his financial service activities under one roof.

Small investors, who abandoned the stock market in the mid-1970s, have returned en masse according to the latest New York Stock Exchange Investor Survey. The typical investor today is younger and has smaller average holdings than his counterpart in 1975, the last time the stock exchange took a reading of America's shareowners. Based on a survey of more than 7,000 homes in the summer of 1980 and updated in the summer of 1981, the total number of stockholders in the country rose to a new record of 32 million people versus the record of 30 million set in 1970.[2]

NEW PRODUCT DEVELOPMENT

New product development in the financial service field is largely intuitive. As has been mentioned, the cost of service development is low compared to the launching costs of new products in the packaged goods field. There is also little expense in dropping a service that proves to be unpopular and unprofitable. This contrasts with the substantial expense of discontinuing a product in the consumer packaged goods field. In the financial service field there is no inventory which must be returned and disposed of at "fire sale" prices.

The attitude in the financial service field is, therefore, that there is no need to do expensive market research when you can offer new services at relatively low financial cost and with little delay in packaging or dropping a service. Try it—if it works, expand distribution to all outlets—if it fails, just discontinue the service.

Among the suppliers of financial services commercial banks are the most active in market research. This has grown out of their need to offer more services to make each banking office more profitable. Mutual funds are beginning to become more market research-oriented since they now must rely on their own direct sale marketing approach and not on the broker/dealer network as in former years. For example, Walter D. Scott, the new president of Investors Diversified Services (IDS) says he will double their spending for market research and product development in order to discover and deliver the investment vehicles customers want instead of those they can be pushed into buying. "We intend to become a customer-driven organization and less of a sales and product-driven company." The company will create specialized financial services targeted at individual groups such as doctors, lawyers, small businesses, and their employees. Scott is aiming at households in the $30,000 to $50,000 income range up from the $20,000 to $40,000 range. This upscale market will give IDS a chance to try direct mail techniques targeted at specific market segments.[3]

Changing competitive trends and chaotic financial markets are forcing insurance companies to become more market-oriented. They are looking to market and new service research to help them diversify into more lucrative sectors of the financial service field. Insurance companies stumbled badly in their first attempt to diversify into the mutual fund field in the late 1960s. Their caution now, and their new emphasis on market research is an attempt to avoid the pitfalls of the past and a recognition of their lack of knowledge of other financial service fields. Despite this caution, many insurance companies continue to be naive. The Prudential/ Bache merger of last year appears to have been unsuccessful so far, largely because of Prudential's lack of expertise and their inability to perceive the real risks and problems in the Bache organization.

Prudential has moved to take a firmer hand in managing the Bache subsidiary. Their recent name change to Prudential/Bache Securities, Inc. reflects Prudential's more direct involvement in the internal affairs of Bache.

Thrift institutions are fighting for survival and lobbying to free themselves from bothersome and restrictive regulations. New product research has been kept in low register while the industry tries to gain help from Washington. The last major new product from the thrifts was the NOW account which revolutionized the checking account business. New banking legislation passed in the fall of 1982 substantially broadened the legal power of thrifts to branch out into other areas of the financial service industry. Under this legislation, thrifts may loan up to 30 percent of their assets as consumer loans and up to 10 percent of their assets as loans to commercial customers. Moreover, thrifts, as well as commercial banks, may now offer a new liquid asset account which the banking bill describes as fully equivalent and competitive to the money market mutual funds that have attracted about $230 billion in new assets over the past ten years. These accounts will carry FDIC deposit insurance up to $100,000 so the public may prefer them to money market mutual funds. Market research and development rushed these new products to market in late 1982.

The entrée of nonfinancial companies should spur market and product research. These companies are targeting their efforts at tapping the lucrative small-income saver and are developing mass programs suitable to their present markets and their established mass merchandising techniques learned over many years of retailing. The expanded IRA and Keogh plan limits are very attractive to Sears and other mass marketers.

A RANDOM SAMPLING OF CURRENT MARKET RESEARCH

Market research activities have been limited but below is a sampling of information about the financial service consumer gleaned from trade publications and company reports issued over the past several years.

Analysis of Bank Customers' Wants

A survey conducted in the summer of 1978 revealed that bank customers rank high the following services:

- automatic payment mechanisms
- credit acceptability
- bank accessibility (they prefer to have banks open on Saturday rather than use an automated teller machine).
- account simplicity[4]

Trust Departments

The consumer's knowledge of the trust functions of his bank are extremely low, compared to his familiarity with other banking services. In a recent survey, only 21 percent of all consumers appeared familiar with bank trust service concepts and only 5 percent with estate planning services.[5] Only 3.5 percent of these consumers have ever used bank trust services, and only 1 percent appear to have ever availed themselves of the bank's estate planning capabilities. In contrast, checking, savings, car loans, and safe deposit services—the traditional banking services—are recognized by 40 percent to 90 percent of all consumers. These are the services that are widely used and that are profitable today.

If we consider bank marketing and advertising budgets, the reason for this becomes clear. The bulk of spending, some 40 to 80 percent of an average bank's marketing budget, is spent on the commercial banking side. Only 2 to 3 percent of an average bank's overall marketing budget is actually devoted to promoting trust services. For banks of under $5 million in size, the total annual marketing budget is usually around $10,300. Using industry averages, the bank with assets under $5 million probably spends about $309 annually marketing trust services. For banks of over $1 billion in size, the total marketing budget for the bank is about $1.65 million—and that is to promote all services in the bank.

Surveys of Usage of Banking Services

In a 1980 survey[6] of consumer usage of financial services, attention was focused on seven banking services as follows:

Checking Accounts

The most commonly used service of financial institutions is the checking account. Almost 96 percent of the households in the consumer panel reported at least one checking account in early 1980. The checking account is somewhat less common in the under-30 age group and in low-income groups. The availability of NOW accounts on a national basis through banks and savings institutions should expand the use of checking by certain groups, as well as reduce the dominance of the commercial bank checking account in the financial affairs of households. The majority of reporting households held more than one bank checking account in 1980. Approximately 44 percent reported one checking account, almost 50 percent had two or three checking accounts, and 6 percent reported four or more accounts. Households with multiple accounts may also use more than one bank. Household groups with the highest frequencies of checking accounts are also the groups which are more likely to hold multiple accounts. For example, households with higher incomes generally report more than one checking account.

Savings Accounts and Certificates of Deposit

Almost 53 percent of the households studied held regular savings accounts in commercial banks in 1980. Approximately the same number reported regular savings accounts in savings and loan associations, while 41 percent had savings balances in credit unions. The regular savings balances in commercial banks were lower than in either savings and loans or credit unions. Fifty-five percent of the regular savers in banks had balances under $1,000, whereas only 35 percent of savings and loan savers and 42 percent of credit union savers reported balances under $1,000. Of those reporting regular savings balances of $5,000 or above, 23 percent held theirs in savings and loan associations, 19 percent in credit unions but only 12 percent of these larger balances were maintained in commercial banks.

Money Market Certificates and Funds

The relative popularity of money market certificates obtained through regular financial institutions was reflected in the survey.

Some 24 percent of all households reported holding the $10,000 minimum money market certificate.

The fact that 72 percent of those reporting money market certificates indicated they had obtained them through a saving and loan association and only 28 percent through a bank is rather unexpected. The fact that banks and savings and loans were aggressive advertisers of these certificates at the time (1980) makes this finding more noteworthy.

Individual Retirement Accounts

Fifteen percent of all households reported an IRA arrangement. The groups with higher income levels and those in the 50- to 60-year-old age category were most heavily represented. Almost one-third of those in the highest income grouping maintained an IRA.

Installment Loans Obtained from Financial Institutions

Household installment borrowing from financial institutions remains quite prevalent as demonstrated by the 41 percent of households indicating they had obtained a nonmortgage loan during the previous 12 months. As would be expected, the proportion of households with installment loans outstanding as of the survey date was somewhat larger, standing at 57 percent of all responding units. Since borrowers obtain funds on a non-installment basis as well, the relatively small differences are more significant than they first appear.

Credit Card Usage by Households

Bank Cards. Bank credit card holdings increased substantially during the last half of the 1970s. Household respondents in 1980 reported holding Visa cards in 47 percent of the cases and MasterCard in 48 percent of the cases. The respective percentages in an earlier (1976) panel survey were 35 percent and 44 percent. National survey data in 1978 indicated that 41 percent of all families held a bank credit card. Visa USA now claims 41.3 million active accounts while Interbank (MasterCard) reports 37 million accounts.

Credit Cards other than Bank or Gasoline Cards. The traditional entertainment and travel cards such as American Express,
Diner's Club, and Carte Blanche were not widely held by the
households surveyed. American Express cards were reported by 10
percent of the households participating in this study. The number
of Diner's Club and Carte Blanche cards was much lower and not
reported in detail. A national survey indicated that 11.2 percent of
family units had such cards in 1978. These cards do not have the
versatility of the bank cards and have always entailed the payment
of an annual charge by the holder.

National data indicate that 45 percent of family units have at
least one national retail card while 24.4 percent have at least once
local retail credit card. Of the households reporting in this study, 39
percent held Sears' cards and 21 percent held Penney's cards.

Gasoline Credit Cards. National survey data indicate that only
35 percent of families held oil company credit cards in 1978, but
the respondents in this study showed an incidence of 57 percent.
This level of holdings is about the same as in 1976. The demo-
graphic characteristics of gasoline credit card holders are very
similar to those of bank and other credit cards.

Household Usage of Electronic Funds Transfer Services

The nation is still on the threshold of the implementation of
electronic funds transfer (EFT) as a replacement for the slow and
expensive movement of currency and paper checks that serves as
our present payments mechanism. One of the major stumbling
blocks to progress in this regard appears to be consumer resistance.
Thus, the survey participants' experience with and attitudes toward
EFT were studied to provide insight into the sources of the public's
resistance to this new technology.

Automated Teller Machines. In spite of the convenience of
automated teller machines (ATM), only 29 percent of the respondents reported ever having used these machines. While this
figure represents a considerable jump from the 9 percent usage
reported in the 1976 survey, automated teller machines have
obviously not been universally adopted by the public. Those who
have used them are primarily under 30 years of age, with annual

incomes over $20,000. A strong inverse relationship exists between age and the use of automated tellers. Only in the under-30 age group was usage greater than 50 percent reported. Experience with the machines dropped precipitously with age to the point that less than one in eight of the respondents over 60 reported having used them. When asked why they did not use automated teller machines, 55 percent of the panel members with access to them reported that present banking facilities were adequate for their purposes that is they felt no need for the service. Suspicion of the new system, the possibility of its malfunction, and risk were relatively minor objections.

Direct Payroll Deposit. Over 30 percent of the sample engaged in direct deposits, up from 21 percent in the 1976 survey. Of that number, 59 percent received direct deposits from their employer, 28 percent received them from Social Security, 19 percent from the military, and 4 percent from other sources. The vast majority of direct deposits were made to bank checking accounts rather than to savings accounts or thrift institutions.

Transfer Services. When asked if they use preauthorized automatic transfers of funds from one type of account to another within the same financial institution, over 25 percent of the panel answered affirmatively, compared to 19 percent in the earlier survey.

No-Cash/Less-Cash Systems. Perhaps the most profound impact of the new technology will be the facilitation of retail sales by the direct electronic funds transfer from customer to store account, sometimes referred to as a "Point of Sales" (POS) or "no cash system." Retailers in particular benefit from this system because check losses are virtually eliminated. Consumers benefit through quick check approval or EFT payment.

When asked how they felt about this new concept, negative responses captured nearly half of the panel responses. Another quarter were neutral, while the remainder liked it. Those who liked it were primarily under 30 years of age, with incomes over $10,000.

Surveys in the Money Management and Investment Fields

Money Market Funds

A 1980 survey found that three out of four money market fund shareholders were males and a majority said they would consider buying other mutual funds if they liquidated their money market accounts. The source of purchase of the money market funds varied between 3.8 percent from six month CD rollovers to 25.4 percent from savings accounts, and 17.6 percent from the sale of stocks, bonds, or mutual funds. The survey noted that 82 percent said they were aware of other mutual funds, this contrasts with only 30 percent awareness several years ago.[7].

The increasing popularity of mutual funds is reflected in another survey conducted by researchers at Purdue University. They analyzed about 1,000 brokerage customers and found that 44 percent owned mutual funds.[8]

Pension Funds and Mutual Funds

The Investment Company Institute (ICI) conducted a survey in mid-1980 of the medium-sized pension market (plans under $10 million in assets) deemed to be prime market targets for mutual fund shares.[9] The survey indicates widely varied perceptions among pension fund administrators and trustees as to which method achieves the best investment results for their pension funds:

	Believe Best Performers Are: (percent)
In-house management	23
Outside investment manager	32
Bank Trust department	25
Insurance company	18
Mutual fund	3

The perception by mid-sized pension fund trustees of mutual fund managers as mediocre sources of investment management services is reflected in the small portion of assets invested in mutual fund shares:

Who Manages Mid-Sized Pension Fund Assets

	Portion of Assets Managed (percent)
Banks	51.6
Insurance companies	19.4
Investment advisor firms	19.9
In–house managers	7.1
Mutual funds	2.0
Total	100.0

It should be pointed out that mutual funds are managed by many investment advisory firms which also manage pension fund assets. Thus a substantial portion of the 19.9 percent indicated above as pension assets managed by investment advisory firms represent mutual fund management companies as well.

Although pension funds continue to favor banks as their investment managers, their performance compared to mutual funds and market indexes compares poorly (see Table 1.1).

Although the surveys show that only three out of ten pension fund administrators were aware of mutual funds, they rate the basic qualities and attributes of mutual funds highly.

Mid-Sized Pension Fund Trustee Ranking of Preferred Attributes

The IPC survey found mid-sized pension trustees considered the following attributes very important:

	Ranking (percent
Investment Expertise of the Manager	84
Performance Compared with Other Advisors	71
Low Expense Ratios	63
Administrative Services	59
Convenience of Not Having to Watch the Portfolio Closely	54
Ease of Asset Allocation Among Differing Investment Objectives	48

Women and Investing

Another ICI survey (conducted in mid-1978)[10] found that nine out of ten wives participate in investment decisions and seven out of ten single and widowed women make their own investment decisions. Women's savings goals differ somewhat from men's:

Women's Savings Goals
(percent)

Travel/vacations	45.2
Future retirement	44.9
Financing children's education	39.0

1971-72 Small Investor Survey

This survey was conducted by the New York Stock Exchange at the height of the bull market. Despite this fact, stocks ranked third, behind real estate and savings as principal investments. It was found that the small investor values the broker relationship, considering him a confidant. Transaction costs were not a deterrent to the small investor. The small investor believed that the big investor does better because of inside information. The small investor was unaware of the protection afforded him under the Securities Industry Protection Corporation.[11]

1980 and 1981 Shareowner Surveys

This survey was the ninth undertaken by the New York Stock Exchange and was conducted in two parts, one in mid-1980 and the other in mid-1981, which updated the 1980 findings. The revised survey shows that shareownership has risen to an all-time record of 32,260,000 stockholders, eclipsing the previous record of 30,850,000 recorded in 1970. The survey indicates that the disenchantment with stocks that was evident in the decline of shareownership by some five million investors between 1970 and 1975 has finally come to an end.

New York Stock Exchange Shareownership Survey[12]

	1970	1975	1981
Shareownership (millions)	30.85	25.27	32.26
Average Age (median)	48	52.5	46
Median Family Income	$13,500	$19,000	$29,200
U.S. Average Income	$8,500	$11,200	$17,700
Median Portfolio Size	NA	$10,000	$4,000

NA-not available.

Public Attitudes toward Investing Alternatives

The basic goals of preserving capital and purchasing power to keep abreast of inflation were revealed by this survey conducted in 1977 and 1978 by the New York Stock Exchange.[13] Seventy percent of respondents were unwilling to take the slightest investment risk.

Attitudes toward Ownership of Investment Vehicles (NYSE)

	Positive Attitude (percent)
Life insurance	92
Savings accounts	86
Home ownership	83
Savings bonds	47
Employee savings plans	34
Savings certificates	34
Real estate (other than home)	30
Tangibles	29
NYSE stocks	27
Employee profit sharing	25
Ownership of closely held firms	19
IRA accounts	16
Mutual funds (stock)	11
Annuities	10
Over-the-counter stocks	9
Preferred stocks	9
Treasury bonds	6

Attitudes toward Ownership of Investment Vehicles (NYSE) (cont.)

	Positive Attitude (percent)
Municipal bonds	5
Convertible securities	5
Treasury bills	5
Corporate bonds	5
Tax free funds	3
Tax shelters	2
Options	1
Warrants	1
Commodity contracts	1

Attitudes toward Various Financial Institutions

	Favorable	Don't Know
Savings banks	67 (percent)	6
Commercial banks	59	7
Life insurance companies	55	8
New York Stock Exchange	44	36
Stock brokerage firms	26	47
Individual stock brokers	26	46
Securities & Exchange Commission	24	51
Commodity exchanges	16	63

Investment Company Institute Public Attitude Study of the Mutual Fund Industry (1971)

This survey revealed that only one out of three households was aware of mutual funds. Mutual fund owners were not aware of mutual fund performance or how mutual funds operate. Non-owners, who claimed to know about mutual funds, did not focus on investment expertise and diversification as key attributes and benefits of mutual fund ownership. The typical fund buyer relied on the broker/dealer salesman for advice.[14]

Finally, advertising agencies have done little research of their own in the financial service area because of the perceived lack of potential in advertising dollars when compared to the consumer package goods business. All of this should change now. Advertising expenditures and effectiveness have plateaued in the packaged goods field and many consumer giants are entering the financial service field with intentions of building strong consumer franchises in the financial service field through advertising.

NOTES

1. Anthony Autin, Jr., Vice President of Pan-American Life Insurance Co., "Product Change: The Challenge of the 1980s", *Best's Review*, July 1980.

2. *Shareownership 1981*, New York Stock Exchange, April 1982.

3. "IDS: Upheaval at the Grandaddy of One-Stop Financial Shopping," *Business Week*, July 13,1981.

4. "How to Find Out What Customers Want From Their Bank," Peter Mears and Frederick Siegel, *The Bankers Magazine*, July-August 1981, pp. 67-77.

5. "How to Use Trust Marketing Research," Joel N. Greene, *Trusts & Estates*, June 1980, pp. 29-36.

6. "Consumer Usage of Financial Services," F. Jerry Ingram and Olin S. Pugh, *The Bankers Magazine*, July-August 1981, pp. 40-53.

7. "Money Market Funds: Interested Investors and Purchasers," *Investment Company Institute* (Research Department), July 1980.

8. "Selling Mutual Funds in Today's Market," Alfred P. Johnson, *Investment Company Institute*, November 8, 1976.

9. "The Retirement Plan Market-A Survey," *Investment Company Institute*, June 1980.

10. "Survey of Working Women," *Investment Company Institute*, April 1979.

11. "Marketing Securities to the Small Investor," *New York Stock Exchange,* 1971-72.

12. "Shareowner Survey: 1981 and 1980," *New York Stock Exchange,* April 1982 and December 1981.

13. "Public Attitudes Towards Investing," *New York Stock Exchange,* June 1978.

14. "The Public's Attitudes Toward Mutual Funds-Awareness, Ownership, and Opinions," *Investment Company Institute,* March 1971.

FIVE

Commercial Banking

Commercial banking has emerged from its monopolistic, paternalistic state into a rapidly changing, highly competitive field trying mightily to expand into allied sectors of the financial service field. Competition is growing in consumer businesses with money funds, and in the commercial loan business with the growth of commercial paper. Although the foregoing is true, much of commercial banking practice is restrictive in nature in the view of many commercial bank competitors. For example, David Silver, president of the Investment Company Institute, recently stated "It is not generally realized that the banking industry, even with the repeal of interest rate ceilings, is the most non-competitive business in the United States. The reason is that the McFadden Act of 1927 restricts national banks to doing business in a single state and the so-called Douglass amendment does the same for the banking activities of bank holding companies. As a result, in 21 states, one banking institution controls at least 20 percent of the banking business in that state."[1]

Commercial banking is among the most regulated segments of the financial service industry. The McFadden Act restricts federally chartered bank branching to that permitted by the individual host state, effectively banning interstate banking. The Glass-Steagall Act bans commercial banks from most investment banking activities.

63

Moreover, banks are subject to many overlapping regulatory authorities including the Federal Deposit Insurance Corporation, the Federal Reserve System, the Comptroller of the Currency, and the Depository Institutions Deregulation Committee, as well as the banking commissioner of each state in which the bank is qualified to do business.

The commercial banking lobby, one of the strongest in Washington, D.C., is currently concentrating on getting Congress to modify many of these restrictive laws and overlapping authorities. Bankers bristle at the competitive inroads made by non-depository institutions into the banking area. Walter B. Wriston, chairman and chief executive officer of Citicorp, says the Shearson/American Express merger plan "makes a total mockery out of Glass-

FIGURE 5.1
Who Does What in Financial Services

	Take Money/ Pay Interest	Check Writing	Loans	Mortgages	Credit Cards	Interstate Branches
Commercial Banks	X	X	X	X	X	
American Express	X	X	X	X	X	X
Merrill Lynch	X	X	X	X	X	X
Prudential	X	X	X	X	X	X
Sears	X	X	X	X	X	X
Beneficial	X	X	X	X	X	X
Transamerica	X	X	X	X		X
Baldwin Piano	X	X	X	X	X	X
RCA			X	X	X	X
Household	X	X	X	X	X	X
Gulf & Western	X	X	X	X	X	X
American General	X	X	X	X		X
Control Data	X		X	X		X
E. F. Hutton	X	X	X			X
Equitable Life	X	X	X	X		X
AVCO			X	X		X
General Electric	X		X	X		X
National Steel	X	X	X	X	X	X
ITT			X	X		X
J. C. Penney					X	X

Steagall. It's driven the final nail in the coffin of bank holding company regulation."[2]

James D. Robinson, III, the chairman of American Express has been realistic but conciliatory in his contacts with bankers. His recent speeches to banking groups have been soothing in tone, filled with platitudes about "partnership", and have stressed how much money banks already make by selling American Express travelers checks and gold charge cards.

Many bankers believe their very existence is threatened by high interest rates and the drain of money to unregulated financial service companies. (see Fig. 5.1) To these bankers American Express is a symbol of the larger issue of decontrol. American Express is widely viewed as the prototype of the company that can offer a variety of financial products without being constrained by regulations, including those regulations intended to protect the customer. Banks, in contrast, are among the most tightly regulated

Money Market	Securities	Insurance	Buy/Rent Real Estate	Cash Management Acct.	Travel Agency/ Service	Car Rental
X	X	X		X	X	
X	X	X	X	X		
X	X	X	X	X		
X	X	X	X	X	X	X
		X				X
X	X	X	X			X
		X	X		X	
		X				X
		X				X
		X	X		X	
X	X	X	X			
		X	X			
X	X	X		X		
X		X		X		
			X		X	
		X				
			X			
		X				
		X	X			

Source: "Old Bank Robbers' Guide to Where the New Money is," Citibank booklet published in 1981.

businesses, with rules that limit the kinds of products they can offer, how much interest they can pay, what proportions of deposits they must keep on reserve, and where they can do business.

Bankers have been advocating decontrol for years. In the three years since Merrill Lynch popularized money market funds and cash management accounts, attracting billions of dollars in deposits from savings accounts, the advocacy has intensified.

In recent months American Express has acquired Shearson Loeb Rhoades Inc., the country's second largest securities brokerage; Prudential Insurance has bought Bache, Halsey, Stuart, Shield, Inc. and Sears, Roebuck & Co., already a major issuer of credit, acquired Dean Witter, Reynolds.

Bankers are sharply divided on what a deregulated banking industry should look like.[3] Big banks like Citibank and Chase Manhattan Bank urge abolishing any restraints imposed on banks that are not imposed on other financial institutions. Smaller banks want to be able to provide the same products American Express and Sears do, but they also are fighting to keep big banks out of their regions.

The so-called independent bankers vigorously oppose decontrol. Many of them would go so far as to impose certain restrictions on nonbank financial institutions. They contend that the money collected by companies like American Express does not get lent again to the housing and agriculture/industries as bank deposits do. They also point out that nonbank deposits are not protected by federal deposit insurance.

Larger regional banks generally favor decontrol, but many urge that the pace of the process be tempered.

EVOLUTION OF MARKETING IN BANKING*

Pre-1950

No understanding or regard for marketing was evidenced in this early development period of the banking industry. Banks felt

---

*This section was adapted from the article "Bank Marketing Strategy–Past, Present and Future," written by Michael P. Sullivan, a bank marketing professional.

they were suppliers of needed services and the public would come to them. Bank buildings were built in the image of Greek temples to impress the public with their strength and durability.

The 1950s

The nation was well into industrial maturity. Ralph J. Cordiner, head of General Electric was calling for business to adopt the marketing concept as a corporate philosophy. Banks were local by orientation and often overseen by strong individual personalities as chief executive officers.

The marketing concept was introduced into banking and the smiling, friendly era was born.

Helpful friendliness was recognized as the key to retail banking. While there still remained many teller cages and long teller lines, bankers were beginning to understand that convenience was the key to the future of retail banking.

Bankers started to rebuild and renovate their facilities. Banks opened many more branches which were built and furnished in comfortable modern style, without teller windows and cages. The goals were to increase lobby traffic and make the teller transaction more pleasant and convenient for the customer. Lobby displays often explained the role of the bank in civic and community affairs.

Later in the decade banks adopted heavy advertising schedules and sales promotion programs to help market services. Much of this advertising promotion relied heavily on the lessons drawn from consumer goods companies such as Procter & Gamble and General Foods. Bankers were now doing more than running the typical small space ads which reported the bank's quarterly and annual earnings. Advertising was geared toward eliminating the feeling of strangeness that customers felt upon entering a bank where no officer was known to customers.

Advertisements for the most part, were institutional except for a few that stressed savings. A photograph of the bank or a line drawing of it often was used in the advertisements. The impressive architecture and the street address of the bank were featured. Art provided by the newspapers from clip art books was used. The design of the ads-headlines, art, copy-was usually provided by the newspaper's art department.

Some banks were beginning to experiment with local television. These advertisements were mostly public service in nature. In banking literature, bankers were relating to one another that television had great impact and that, while they were cautious, they were interested in seeking ways to use television effectively.

In the 1950s bankers were more comfortable with public relations than with advertising, so, consequently they emphasized public relations more than advertising.

. Personal selling was not widely recognized as being necessary. In fact, bankers went out of their way to avoid being accused of selling. Rather than selling, bankers prefered to use the term "business development."

The 1960s

Institutional advertising was replaced by product advertising in the 1960s. As competition continued to increase, banks began the banking innovation era. Bank of America offered customers 350 separate financial services. In the 1950s savings had been the only banking service advertised. A decade later a range of retail services was promoted, including checking accounts, automobile loans, college tuition loans, and personal trust services. The hottest product of the 1960s was the bank-issued credit card with its pre-approval credit lines.

There were then (and are now) two major national bank cards-Bank Americard (VISA) and Master Charge (MasterCard). Each is issued by individual local banks operating under a franchise arrangement with a national bank card organization. Both of these national bank cards experienced rapid growth during this period. There were no restrictions on the use of mailing lists to send cards to prospects on an unsolicited basis. (Laws now prohibit unsolicited mailings and make it unlikely that a third competitor could enter the market in the same way and grow as rapidly.)

Creativity in bank advertising became more pronounced in the 1960s. Advertisements were more appealing. Design and layout elements for newspaper advertising improved. Testimonials of employees and customers were used frequently in bank advertising. Premiums of home appliances, books, luggage, and stuffed animals figured prominently in bank advertising. Banks used these premiums to reward customers for opening new accounts or adding to existing ones.

Bankers' attitudes and comprehension about marketing changed in the 1960s. They began to realize that marketing was a lot more than smiling, friendly tellers. Corporate identity programs became popular in the late 1960s. Bankers realized the image of the bank was communicated in many ways and they needed to plan and coordinate this image.

While the idea of customer convenience began in the late 1950s, it flourished in the 1960s. Time-saving customer services like the drive-up window began to appear. Customers were asked, in surveys, what they thought about the bank, and the bank responded to those answers by improving services. The concept of the "personal banker", a consumer account officer assigned to help a specific number of customers, became popular.

Bankers were beginning to understand the concept of market segmentation and, late in the decade, promotions began to be directed to the women's market, the mature market, the family market, and the high income upscale market.

During this period, advertising agencies were used by banks to plan and execute advertising campaigns, a departure from using advertisements created by newspaper art departments or television production departments. Marketing budgets were now large enough that agencies could be adequately compensated by media placement fees.

Bankers realized that the new-accounts officer, seated at a desk in the lobby, had an opportunity to cross-sell many of the bank's services. There was plenty of opportunity for cross-selling. The average household used only 1.7 bank services, very low compared with the many services available, such as savings accounts, credit cards, installment loans, revolving credit, mortgage loans, and tuition loans.

On the commercial or wholesale side of the banking business, there was considerable progress. Sales techniques borrowed from industry were being used by banks. Programs for the training and development of bank officers who solicit commercial accounts, were used by all banks. Some commercial bank advertising was being placed mainly in regional and local business magazines.

The 1970s

The bank marketing profession changed dramatically in the 1970s. Marketing positions in banks were being filled by those with more formal education, more experience, and an awareness of what marketing could do. Specialties emerged in large banks such as advertising manager, public relations officer, research director, and sales promotion manager. More community banks were accepting marketing as an organizational imperative.

A major influence on bank marketing in the 1970s was the advent of electronic funds transfer systems. These included automated teller machines, cash dispensing machines, direct deposit of payroll, pay-by-phone systems, point-of-sale systems, credit and debit cards, preauthorized funds transfer, and the automated clearinghouse. Automation literally and figuratively changed the face of banking. The alternatives available to banks now had become almost limitless. Depending on legal restrictions, bank terminals or shared systems were apt to be found anywhere— depots, airports, employee breakrooms, college campuses, kiosks in shopping centers—even reaching into the home via cable television.

In the 1970s, bankers experienced a new source of competition, nonbank competitors such as money market mutual funds which had grown to over $230 billion by 1982.

Budgets for bank advertising increased. As a rule of thumb, advertising expenditures of banks generally were one-tenth of 1 percent of a bank's deposits. For example, a bank with $100 million in deposits had a $100,000 advertising budget. With additional money available for advertising agencies, bank advertising became much more interesting in the 1970s. All types of visually appealing advertising were used—cartoon characters, celebrities, dramatizations, and symbolism. Automated banking was the subject of almost half the bank advertisements.

The packaging of bank services—the tying together of free checking, pre-authorized credit, credit cards, discounted travel or entertainment, and traveler's checks—swept the country in the early 1970s. These packaged programs were advertised heavily to gain market share and increase the household use of services.

Agency relationships changed as the 1970s wore on. Bank advertising managers looked at creative boutiques for increased creativity and cost savings. Some experimented with their own in-house advertising agencies, which were justified by the saving the agency media placement fees. This arrangement did not however work out in the long run and most in-house agencies have been closed.

Bank public relations changed dramatically as well. The positions were staffed by better educated, more professional managers. Departments were expanded and the function was broadened. In addition to media relations, the public relations person often was responsible for community affairs, public affairs, internal communications, government affairs, and investor relations.

Personal selling by banks in the 1970s took on a new role. In the 1960s bankers learned sales techniques, in the 1970s they learned about human motivation as part of the sales effort. Many banks purchased the services of professional sales consultants to conduct sales seminars, international workshops, and self-instruction sales programs and to consult in sales management (the identification of prospects, and determining sales call routes and frequencies).

The 1980s

Advertising, public relations, and personal selling will change dramatically by the end of the 1980s. Banking itself is destined for major changes due to economic, technological, and structural reasons. Among the major possibilities:

- banks or bank holding companies will be permitted to establish deposit-accepting offices across state lines
- the total number of commercial banks in the United States will shrink dramatically in number through mergers and acquisitions, while the total number of banking offices will expand perhaps four-fold
- technology, specifically electronic funds transfer system will become a major force in breaking down the barriers to interstate banking. In-home electronic banking will become the dominant form for delivering personal banking services
- extensive competition will result from nontraditional sources providing financial services to bank customers.

Costs will continue to escalate for mass media. Media innovations and market segmentation by banks will provide some cost relief. Direct marketing will replace the use of mass media as the major vehicle in a campaign. In-home electronic terminals will carry advertising messages on a selective basis. Advertising content in the early 1980s will be increasingly pretested, tied more to the profile of the reader/viewer/listener audience. Response devices will be a part of almost all advertising, helping the advertiser to justify the expenditure. Incentives of all types will be offered to attract customers. Some types of banking services offered today have severe restrictions about gifts or premiums offered by the bank. These restrictions may be eliminated.

Public relations in the 1980s will be marked by more planning, more positioning of the distinctive image of each bank, and a higher awareness of the value of public relations to the banking organization.

In an era of mergers and acquisitions, corporate identity programs will become increasingly important, as banks seek to develop a consistent image among the many entities of the bank. Banks will spend more time positioning and re-positioning the image of a bank in the public's mind to capitalize on each bank's unique strengths versus the competition. This could take the form of more convenient locations, faster auto loans, more liberal lines of credit, or better trust services.

"Niche banking" will become the buzzword of the 1980s as banks try to find a unique niche and then position themselves to meet the public's expectations.

Banks which have traditionally spent most of their marketing dollars attracting and retaining customers, will begin to devote a large share of their marketing budgets on internal programs to improve employee efficiency, service, and loyalty. Closed circuit television will become the major means of reaching employees, with company-produced video programs reaching into the employees' homes.

Personal selling in banking will attempt to move to a consultative selling relationship. Developing a more personal and ongoing relationship with clients will receive major emphasis. Officers with responsibility for maintaining customer relations will become more sophisticated in planning calls to provide the customer with information between sales calls. Sales presentations will be more visually attractive and will be in keeping with the image of the banking organization.

Concurrent with these trends will be a renewed emphasis on long range planning, market analysis and the development of controls to improve long-term profitability and market penetration.

The calling officer will become a major part of the concept of niche banking. The calling officer will be backed up with an array of impressive data support systems to make the cells cost effective and provide instantaneous customer information. Trust banking and the unique relationship role it provides may also become the core marketing relationship of the 1980s.[4]

COMMERCIAL BANKING IN THE CONTEXT OF THE FINANCIAL SERVICE INDUSTRY

Commercial banking is the most powerful individual segment of the financial service field. Because of restrictive regulation, however, the development and expansion of commercial banking has been constrained, with banking services limited to the relatively narrow field of deposit/loan/trust activities. If these regulations are removed or substantially modified commercial banks would expand their horizons considerably and would probably more closely resemble the British and European prototypes. Banking services in western Europe already embrace most of the financial service field. The European commercial bank in effect achieved the financial supermarket by evolution many decades ago. In England, for example, an individual transacts his stock purchases, arranges for management of his investment account, as well as maintains his cash and checking accounts, all at a convenient branch of his bank. If he is interested in buying a new issue of a company the merchant bank affiliate of his bank could handle the transaction as an investment banker. When he travels a branch of his bank will be nearby whether he is going to Bombay or Surrey. The British clearing banks have more bank branches than any other system in the world including that of the United States. If his company has need for long-term investment funds for expansion the bank could satisfy his requirements either by a long-term loan or through an investment banking flotation arranged by his bank's merchant banking affiliate.

It may not be long before Americans can enjoy the same conveniences and services that the British have long taken for granted. Several U.S. banks have found loopholes in the banking regulations which permit them to offer discount brokerage services. In one case Security Pacific Bank will offer broker services in conjunction with Fidelity Brokerage Services. In another case Bank of America purchased Schwab, a major discount broker, for 2.2 million Bank of America common shares valued at about $53 million. Bank of America said it believes its purchase of Schwab did not violate the Glass-Steagall Act of 1933 because Schwab simply executes orders and is not involved in underwritings or taking positions in stock, activities which banks are specifically prohibited from engaging in under the Glass-Steagall Act.

Bank Management and Organization

Bank management is arranged in broad service categories with individual managers handling each service area. Typically bank management is divided between commercial and consumer, domestic and international. Strategic planning is a staff function controlled and directed by top management. Product or service managers usually arrange for new service product ideas to be launched.

NEW PRODUCT LAUNCHINGS

One might think that commercial banks have fairly sophisticated market research and new product development programs. It is logical to assume advanced new product programs for most of the money center banks. Actually, little ongoing research is conducted. Most new product launchings are based on informed hunches. As in other areas of the financial service field, the cost of mistakes or failures in new product launchings is relatively small and thus it makes sense to launch a new product on a limited branch-by-branch basis as a sort of "trial balloon." If successful the new service idea is extended to all of the branches, if not it can be discontinued with minimal losses. Most new service ideas are basically refinements of the computer software capability of the bank, so to launch new service involves at most a $50,000 to $100,000 software "tool up" and some additional promotional expenses. Staffing of the new service is usually done by assigning personnel temporarily to the project in the introductory period, including personnel to develop sales literature and a procedures manual for the new service. If all goes well the bank then introduces the service throughout the system with appropriate additional staffing as needed.

This ease of entry has led to a proliferation of new services offered by banks. Several hundred services may be offered in very large banks, with the number of services offered growing geometrically. The proliferation of services causes problems. Many "how to?" questions arise in the branches. How does the bank manage these new service areas and provide complete information to the interested customer on the workings of these various services?

Commercial banks have tried to address themselves to this problem by developing a form of consumer "ombudsman" in the concept of the personal banker. The personal banker is one way that an increasing number of commercial bank are responding to the "I am an individual" consumer. Eventually thrift institutions will adopt this mode of organization to sell financial services. The personal banker, assigned to each retail customer, opens new accounts and cross-sells bank services, makes loans and provides financial consultation, cuts "red tape" when problems arise and is available to help the customer. Personal banking will continue to grow in the 1980s despite the large front-end investment necessary to implement it correctly. This growth will occur mainly to support cross-selling, a must for financial institutions in the 1980s. It is a way to credibly position the bank as a personal, human institution. Banks have typically staffed the personal banker position with relatively untrained personnel who eventually move up in the bank heirarchy. The personal banker is viewed in some banks as a part of their junior executive training program. The turnover in the personal banker ranks at some banks averages every six months. This can be very upsetting to a regular bank customer. It leaves valued customers to fend for themselves during changeover periods, and then to face the necessity of adapting to inexperienced replacements. The inevitability of turnover is demoralizing to the bank customer. The basic concept of the personal banker is sound from the point of view of the bank customer and from the point of view of the bank's desire to expand service and profits— what is needed is the upgrading of the position to a line position with additional compensation incentives, making it attractive as a career opportunity. In other words, the personal banker should occupy as important a role as the individual stock broker in the securities firms. Most investors regard their stock broker as their personal confidant and this relationship is important in expanding the services offered by the firm. As commercial banks expand into more areas of financial service they will be forced to develop the customer service representative—the personal banker—as a full-time career post, so that the system works for both the bank and the consumer.

The product mix in the commercial banking business is broad, involving a wide range of services for consumer and commercial needs. These include checking accounts and deposits, consumer and corporate loans, trust services, pension fund management and investment advisory, credit cards, automated teller machines, Keogh and IRA savings plans, international and domestic money transfers, government securities trading and investment banking services where permitted (including private placements, municipal bond underwritings, and mergers and acquisitions). With the new banking legislation enacted by Congress in 1982, banks can also now offer money market-type liquid asset accounts.

Nonetheless, the appetite for new products continues to grow. Commercial banks would like to broaden their product mix to include the management of common stock mutual funds , investment banking in the field of underwriting corporate bond and stock issues, interstate banking, and more flexible electronic funds transfer.

Banks already are active in the mortgage loan field but restrict most of their loans to commercial office buildings, apartment houses and manufacturing and warehousing facilities.

According to a national survey of banks retail banking will be looking more seriously at cultivating a deposit base in the consumer market.[5] Banks will focus more of their attention on carving out a significant portion of the expanding consumer financial services market for themselves. The survey of bankers was conducted in 50 states in 1979 by Financial Shares Corporation, in conjunction with Market Shares Corporation. The survey found that 71 percent of the nation's top banking executives believe that in the 1980s consumer customers will contribute a greater proportion to the deposit and loan mix than they do now. Most of the bank executives surveyed felt that the consumer will become more important to banking in the early part of the decade.

However, 49 percent of the banks believe they will lose consumer market share to other types of financial service institutions, such as Sears and Merrill Lynch. The survey found that a very high proportion of banks now offer consumer services including:

	Percent
Direct deposit of Social Security	100
Six month money certificates	97
Regular savings	97
Individual Retirement Accounts	93
Credit cards	89
Direct payroll deposits	85
Eight year certificates	84
Small saver certificates	78
Automatic funds transfer	74
Automated teller machines	54
Debit cards	33

The survey company recommended the following approaches to meet the strong competition of the 1980s:

Planning—Take the necessary time to plan long-, intermediate-, and short-range marketing goals and objectives.

Research—Through proper planning and research, get to know the market and the products most needed by customers that can be offered for a profit.

Positioning—Set your bank's goals and objectives to correspond with your positioning strategy.

TABLE 5.1
The Changing Deposit Mix at Commercial Banks
(in billions of dollars)

Year	Demand Deposits	Percent	Passbook Savings Deposits	Percent
1950	117	70	28	17
1955	141	68	38	18
1960	156	61	55	22
1965	184	49	93	25
1970	247	43	99	17
1975	324	34	160	17
1980	432	28	201	13
1982	364	20	297	16

Note: Time deposits exclude large ($100,000 and over) negotiable certificates deposit. Breakdown between time deposits and passbook savings deposits estimated for year prior to 1965. Percentages calculated on the basis of total assets.

Source: FDIC Annual Reports and Federal Reserve Bulletin; figures are stated as of year end.

Product Design and Pricing—Analyze each of your products and change if necessary to make them fit the market you seek to capture. This should include reevaluation of packaging and pricing.

Training—Proper asset management includes proper placement, supervision, training and retraining, and monitoring.

Advertising—The quality and content of bank advertising must keep pace to carry out the identity and positioning strategies.

Consumer preferences in banking

In summary, the various surveys indicate that the following are the major priorities to the consumer of banking services:

Time Deposits	Percent	Large-size Certificates of Deposit	Percent	Other Liabilities including capital	Percent
8	5	0	0	14	8
12	6	0	0	18	8
18	7	0	0	27	10
39	11	16	4	43	11
110	19	26	5	94	16
202	21	101	10	178	18
321	21	238	15	347	23
342	19	360	20	457	25

- high interest returns with low costs
- a variety of services under one roof
- convenience—many branches and convenient hours in the evening and weekends
- service—friendly, informed, people-oriented banks. The personal banker is a meaningful concept if it can be made to work.
- consumers prefer to stay with a bank even when that relationship is less than perfect. Brand loyalty is strong. It is very difficult to get a consumer to switch banks..

Consumers are becoming much more knowledgeable in perceived value. Even though many of the industry's new products have been dictated by government, they nonetheless improve service delivery, and benefits and, if priced and marketed properly, can produce profits.

PRICE STRATEGIES

Price strategies involve combinations of specific fees, interest rates on loans, and the interest earned on compensating balances.

Most price decisions are based on cost plus a profit. However, banks have become more market-oriented in their pricing and use projections of market demand at different fee levels to determine the ultimate fee to be charged. The central mechanism for computing price is the prime rate, which sets the interest rate to be charged to the best customers for loans. Frequently, banks will use the federal funds rate plus a premium in pricing decisions involving very large customers. The federal funds rate is the interbank lending rate and effectively represents the real cost of additional funds to the bank.

Fees charged by the trust division historically have been set low in relation to cost, as a "loss leader," with the objective of retaining or gaining loan business by providing trust and custodian services on a below-cost basis. More recently banks have increased fees on trust department services in order to improve investment management and ultimately performance. Pension fund management used to be dominated by bank trust departments but with the passage of ERISA, more and more corporations are transferring pension fund management to more adroit money managers as mandated by the strict "prudent man" rule contained in ERISA. In order to meet this competition, banks have had to hire more top level securities analysts and managers and accordingly must look to higher fees to finance the effort. Banks used to charge only one-hundredth of 1 percent fee for asset management, they now charge one-quarter of 1 percent or more.

PLACE STRATEGIES

Most distribution of bank services is through the bank-owned premises in the form of full service branches, or, alternatively, through franchising arrangements or other informal agreements with individual banks making up a bank's correspondent network.

To provide the limited service possible in the interstate market, banks maintain offices which can supply all but deposit service in out-of-state locations. Thus large banks, through their holding companies, have nonbanking offices around the country which provide just about every banking service except taking deposits. Manufacturers Hanover Trust, for example, has more than

700 such offices in 28 states. Citibank has offices in 40 states. These banks are ready to move rapidly when and if the restrictions on interstate banking are lifted.

As has been mentioned, many banks wholesale their services through a correspondent banking network, especially in the trust and money management areas. Banks also wholesale loan accounts where the amount exceeds the legal or practical loan limits set at a particular bank.

In recent years, the big money center banks have put renewed emphasis on expanding their retail business by putting a new emphasis on improving service. For both big and small banks, the "retail" or consumer side of the business loses money or, at best, is barely profitable. Retail banking, that is, checking accounts, savings accounts, auto loans, consumer loans—the banking aimed at the average person—is considered an essential market for banks. It provides the funds to help banks build a deposit base and, in some cities at least, it can be a profitable source of interest income and service fees. But retail banking in New York and other large cities depends on a branch system that today proves increasingly burdensome as wages, rents, and utility bills keep going up. At the same time, the market that retail banking serves expands little, reflecting the relatively slow growth of center cities. Competition has been intense, coming not only from commercial banks but savings banks and savings and loan associations as well. The profit squeeze has forced branch closings and a slowdown in openings. Bankers admit that retail banking in large cities has alienated many customers by subjecting them to long lines and poor service. Bankers are convinced that automated teller machines are the logical long-term answer to the problems of retail banking, but they are not sure the consumer agrees.

Most banks are cautiously watching the outcome of Citibank's foray into automated teller machines. Convenience is widely thought to play a critical role in attracting retail customers. Hence, Citibank's machines, most of which operate 24 hours a day, 7 days a week have added a new element to the battle for the consumer dollar. If Citibank does make sharp inroads in existing market shares of retail banking, some banks may be forced to make a heavy investment in machines of their own. According to some bankers, the competitive pressure from Citibank and the general environment for retail banking—or both—could cause some banks to de-emphasize consumer banking operations. Chase Manhattan Bank, for example, has already decided to de-emphasize "trying to be all things to all people" and, instead, is concentrating on consumers with high or growing incomes or those who, like some retired persons and members of some ethnic groups, tend to keep large balances in their accounts or who otherwise are willing to pay for bank services. While plans to market services to these select consumers (such as doctors) are in the works, Chase has already begun centralizing, in three Manhattan branches, services for consumers with high incomes or large assets. It has also discouraged holders of small checking accounts, considered unprofitable, from banking in the branches. Bankers Trust, in a similar vein, sold all of its branches in 1980 in order to concentrate exclusively on developing wholesale banking.

The need of consumers for more rapid service is encouraging their acceptance of the money machines. For example, a national consumer study in 1979, sponsored by the Food Marketing Institute, found that 42 percent of the respondents expressed interest in having banking facilities (presumably automated teller machines) inside supermarkets.

Except for the time saving benefit, automated banking would not stand much of a chance. After all, who wants to do business with a machine? Nevertheless, certain automated services have already assumed important roles in financial institutions' delivery systems and the key reason why is perceived time scarcity. With these machines, consumers are being asked to radically change behavior—to switch to doing business with a machine. They are asked to learn which buttons, among a sea of buttons, to punch. But the automated machine, with its time-saving and flexible properties, is grudgingly winning consumer adoption in a number of markets around the country. The irony of the automated tellers is the trend of long lines of consumers waiting patiently for a free machine to conduct their banking transactions. So we have progress of sorts—transposing long teller lines from inside the bank to long lines waiting for a machine!

A number of companies already are eliminating paychecks and transmitting payroll information by magnetic tape to an automated clearinghouse (ACH), an organization that combines, sorts, and distributes payment orders in machine-readable form. The employee provides his company with the name of his bank. The ACH then distributes the tape to each bank involved. It is argued that direct payroll deposits cost the employer the benefit of the float. Nonetheless, companies like Xerox, IBM, and NCR have discovered they save more money by eliminating check-based payrolls than they lose in float. The same economics work for the consumer. If a man earns $20,000 a year, lost time to cash a check costs him or his firm 18 minutes going to and from the bank office, plus another six minutes waiting on line for the teller resulting in an implicit cost of $5.00 per transaction compared to 40 cents for electronic transfers.

With inflation viewed as a "fact of life" and likely to stay, consumers in increasing numbers are perceiving the need to manage more intelligently their financial affairs. Except in the case of their wealthiest customers, commercial banks have generally ignored this need in the past, failing in the process to be the full-service banks they claim to be. The result is that most consumers turn to accountants, attorneys, insurance companies, brokerage houses, friends, and relatives for help. What most consumers need today is a "financial quarterback," who can help them manage their financial affairs and build a coordinated financial plan. More and more commercial banks will attempt to fill this need in the 1980s, often using the "personal banker" operating in cooperation with or through the trust department.

A group of banks (representing $200 billion in combined assets) agreed in early 1982 to study ways to share their 2,500 automated teller machines, so that customers could obtain cash from any one of them simply by inserting the proprietary debit cards issued by each bank for use with its own machines. That group is only one of more than a dozen contenders in the race to build such networks. Another ATM network is being organized by Chase Manhattan Bank and Rocky Mountain Bank Card System, the credit card processing arm of Colorado National Bank. Bank of America is considering joining this group along with 28 other major banks.

Bank regulations not only limit branch banking to the regulations imposed by the host state but they also dictate strict conditions for the opening or closing of individual branches. Banks must demonstrate that a branch is unprofitable in order to justify closing a branch. Alternatively, a bank must demonstrate pro forma profitability for a proposed new branch in order to gain approval from state banking authorities to open that new branch. The intent of these regulations is to preserve banking services and thereby protect the consumer from arbitrary cessation of banking facilities.

Be that as it may, the reach of distribution facilities to the banking consumer falls far short of ideal in many areas. For example, on the west side of Manhattan, a growing and affluent residential and retail area of New York City, not one branch office of Irving Trust Company exists. A banking customer of Irving must resort to considerable inconvenience to conduct his banking business. By contrast, on the east side of Manhattan, Irving maintains three banking offices for the convenience of its customers located in that area.

Federal law, with some minor exceptions, prohibits banks from operating across state lines. But banks have managed to get around most of the prohibitions against interstate banking by setting up holding companies. Most of these holding companies have formed nonbank financial subsidiaries, such as consumer finance companies, that have offices across the country.

Manufacturers Hanover, as aforementioned, has 700 non-banking offices in 28 states. These offices offer savers small-denomination certificates that are different from deposits. Only banks are permitted to accept deposits. Now even this barrier seems to be crumbling as some of the major banking institutions have begun to search for ways in which they can legally solicit out-of-state consumer deposits, or, as in the case of Manufacturers Hanover, funds that very closely resemble deposits.

Regional banks

In all of the turmoil affecting banking no where is the impact expected to be as great as with the regional banking concerns. Regional banks, cautious by tradition, are revamping their former roles and searching for new niches in the banking system in the face of new rules and competition.

Regional banks have long been important as links between the giant money center banks and thousands of small community banks. But deregulation and stiffer competition means these banks must develop new strategies. The competition is coming from big banks and national financial services giants such as Prudential/Bache and Sears/Dean Witter Reynolds. Interstate mergers of troubled savings institutions into commercial banks is enhancing competition and is likely to force many small community banks into mergers.

Some regional banks already have moved to restructure their retail banking. They are reorganizing their sprawling branch systems that once worked like powerful magnets for savings and checking deposits but have become more costly and less profitable to operate. Philadelphia's Girard Co., for example, with $4.8 billion in assets, has reduced its full-service branches by 20 percent in three years. Automated tellers have replaced humans. Mini-branches have opened at new locations. These measures have increased Girard's market penetration, (number of households with accounts), by nearly 50 percent, while its work force has held steady. The bank is generating new fee income with new transaction charges and services such as bill paying by telephone. The bank's transaction revenues rose by 35 percent to about $8 million in 1981. Such income has become especially important because the high cost of borrowed or "purchased" money, such as large certificates of deposits, often has made bank lending less profitable.

Banc One in Columbus, Ohio has become a leader in specialized services. It contracted to process cash management accounts for nine brokerage firms, which are prevented by regulation from issuing checks. Banc One handles more checks for Merrill Lynch alone, than for all its regular Ohio banking customers. Banc One expected to take in $21 million in processing fees in 1982, up 33 percent from the year before.

First Tennessee National Corp. exploited its location in Memphis, the headquarters of Federal Express. Employing the services of that overnight courier, First Tennessee began an ambitious national check processing service in the fall of 1981. Promising that it could clear checks in one day First Tennessee signed up bank clients eager to reduce their float, or money due on uncleared checks, and get fast access to their cash.

Other regional bankers have decided to move outside regional boundaries to offset lackluster business at home. Philadelphia's Provident National, in the economically stagnant northeast, sold its factoring, leasing and title insurance subsidiaries and, in 1979, began investing $85 million of the proceeds in regional banks elsewhere.

PROMOTION STRATEGIES

Bank promotion places primary reliance on advertising and premiums (gifts) for the development of such consumer services as checking accounts, loans, credit cards, and automated teller machines. Bank advertising expenditures average about one-tenth of 1 percent of deposits which for a billion dollar bank means an annual advertising budget of about $1 million, relatively small by comparison with consumer goods industries.

On the other hand, bank advertising campaigns can stress institutional purposes as well as creating a distinctive image. For example, Chemical Bank launched a $3 million campaign in early 1982 stressing their "heritage of innovation." Each advertisement in the series emphasizes a different element in this heritage—in lending, financial services, and international banking. The campaign is aimed at the top management of the Fortune 1000 companies.

Banks rely on personal selling for promotion of wholesale and investment banking services including corporate loans, trust services, and cash management. Publicity is a very effective promotion vehicle for financial services, especially banks, because the banking public tends to read news accounts and opinions about the world of finance carefully. Publicity in the form of published articles can break through the perceptual screen most consumers have in areas of intangible values, that is, they can create an image of the bank in the public's mind.

Statement mailers are a popular promotion item. Banks also use a substantial amount of sales promotion devices, such as gifts for opening new accounts or adding to old accounts, or for bringing in new accounts by referral. Premiums and other sales promotion tools are used extensively in the launching of new bank branches.

An important aspect of bank promotion is to project a

distinctive image. The positioning statement articulates in writing what the bank is, what makes it distinctive, the role of the parent company, corporate objectives and communication goals and the words that best describe the bank. Visuals are important in conveying a distinctive image. Thus promotion material should include elements of architecture, landscaping, product designing, and the physical appearance and attitudes of the employees—from the receptionist and the tellers to top management.

Danny R. Arnold, a marketing professor at Mississippi State University, suggests this eight step approach for bank advertising:

1) review the external situation—external threats and opportunities
2) review internal situation—internal strength and weaknesses
3) review objectives, strategy and tactics
4) determine advertising objectives
5) develop advertising strategy
6) determine advertising tactics
7) implement campaign plans
8) evaluate advertising effectiveness.

In major efforts to reposition their marketing strategies, two New York banking organizations have begun programs to solicit deposits from consumers across the United States.

Citicorp, the nation's biggest banking company, began by mailing letters to 150,000 of its credit card customers in 15 states, offering them consumer certificates of deposit, with a minimum account size of $3,000. If the test mailing proves successful, Citicorp will expand the campaign nationally, using direct mail.

The Chase Manhattan Corporation, the nation's third largest banking company, ran advertisements in the *Miami Herald*, soliciting deposits. No decision has yet been made about continuing the campaign, although Chase is planning to open a so-called industrial bank in Florida that would be able to accept deposits from consumers as well as businesses.

NOTES

1. "Report to Members," *Mutual Fund Forum*, published by the Investment Company Institution, July 1980.

2. Money Inc.—Wall Street Merger may basically change U.S. Financial System," *Wall Street Journal*, April 22, 1981.

3. "Regional Banks Search for a Niche in Face of New Rules, Competition," *Wall Street Journal*, February 1982.

4. "Bank Marketing Strategy—Past, Present, and Future," Michael P. Sullivan, *The Bankers Magazine*, July/August 1981.

5. "Retail Banking in the 80s—A Smaller Slice of a Bigger Pie," Robert F. Benzer, *Bank Marketing*, December 1979, pp. 21–24.

SIX

The Thrift Industry

In October 1982, Congress approved landmark legislation to subsidize the nation's ailing savings institutions and give them broad new lending powers similar to those of commercial banks.

The legislation also authorized commercial banks, along with savings institutions, to offer a new type of federally insured account nearly identical to the high yield money market mutual funds.

Commercial banks, represented by the American Bankers Association, have fought for years to keep savings institutions from offering consumer and commercial loans, traditionally the domain of the commercial banks. They gave in on this issue, however, partly in exchange for the right to offer the new money market account. The new money market accounts experienced explosive growth in early 1983, reaching $250 billion in assets in less than two months of their availability.

The legislation gives federal regulators the power to issue government-backed promissory notes to bolster the net worth of the nation's more than 4,500 thrift institutions, which have suffered heavy losses as a result of high interest rates.

For the first time savings institutions (including credit unions) would be permitted to make consumer, commercial, and agricultural loans as well as to continue issuing the real estate mortgage loans that have been the mainstay of their investments; commercial and agricultural loans, up to 10 percent of assets and consumer loans, up to 30 percent of assets, would be phased in over the next several years.

Savings and loan associations and mutual savings banks lost $6.4 billion in deposits in 1981. By 1981 year-end, 801 institutions, with $167 billion in assets, were at or below three percent of net worth, the level at which they would qualify for the government-backed promissory notes to bolster their net worths. The year 1981 saw more than 300 mergers, more than double the total in the year before; estimates indicate that mergers in 1982 may have exceeded 500.

The legislation also contains a provision that overturns state bans on "due-on-sale" clauses in mortgage loan contracts. Many financial institutions have been eager to call in their old mortgages on homes when they are sold and issue new loans at the current high market rates, now averaging more than 15 percent.

THE STRUCTURE OF THE INDUSTRY

The thrift industry is divided into three segments: savings and loan associations, mutual savings banks and credit unions (see Table 6.1).

Savings and loan associations represent the largest, most widespread, and most rapidly growing segment of the thrift industry. Savings and loans can be federally chartered or operate under state charters, assets of the two types are divided about equally between the two forms. Widespread branching occurs in western and southern portions of the country through the use of holding companies. In addition to state versus federal charters, savings and loans can be divided into mutual or shareowner owned. Savings and loans have $714 billion in assets with about 80 percent of these assets invested in mortgages. State laws generally limit investments of savings and loans primarily to residential mortgages with 80 percent the usual required minimum.

Mutual savings banks are a special variety of thrift organization growing out of the need to provide "safe harbors" for seaman's

TABLE 6.1
Growth of Thrift Institutions
(total assets in billions of dollars)

Year	Savings & Loans	Mutual Savings Banks	Credit Unions
1971	206.0	89.4	21.1
1972	243.1	100.6	24.7
1973	271.9	106.7	28.3
1974	295.5	109.6	31.9
1975	338.2	121.1	38.0
1976	391.9	134.8	45.2
1977	459.2	147.3	54.1
1978	523.5	158.2	62.6
1979	579.0	163.4	65.9
1980	629.7	171.8	71.7
1981	663.8	175.6	77.7
1982	714.0	180.5	83.6

Source: Statistical Work Book for Members, 1979 as updated, Investment Company Institute.

earnings and to prevent squandering by seaman after returning from long voyages. The eastern seaboard,in the heyday of sailing ships, abounded with dens of iniquity to entice the seaman to part with his hard earned bounty. To prevent this "shanghaiing" of sailors, public spirited individuals took the lead in setting up convenient savings banks near the docks and paymasters of the ships. Thus, most savings banks are mutual and located in the cities of the eastern seaboard. Their names evoke a link to the nautical past—Seaman's Savings Bank, Anchor Savings Bank, East River Savings Bank and Bowery Savings Bank to mention a few giants in New York City. Most mutual savings banks have state charters. Mutual savings banks have about $180 billion in assets with about 60 percent invested in residential mortgages, 10 percent in commercial real estate and the balance in bonds. Savings banks are not as restricted as savings and loans with regard to required mortgage loans.

Credit unions are the third type of thrift organization. Credit unions require some common bond of membership such as place of employment, occupation, or residence, a requirement that has severely restricted their growth. Credit unions are the smallest of the thrifts with only about $84 billion in assets.

Of the approximately 23,000 credit unions, three-fifths are federally chartered and the balance have state charters and all are mutually owned. The investments of credit unions are restricted primarily to consumer loans but are now permitted in the home improvement and home mortgage area also; credit unions may lend only to their own members.

Disintermediation

The thrifts have suffered over the past ten years from the loss of deposits to higher yielding direct or indirect investment media. The mortgage portfolios of thrifts are long-term in nature and the average yield on portfolio investments ranges between 7 and 8 percent while the cost of funds (deposits), which are short-term in nature, fluctuates with the money market rates which have been above 10 percent for the past several years. Under Federal Reserve regulations (Regulation Q), thrifts may not pay more than 5.5 percent on passbook savings accounts. Accordingly, individuals have withdrawn their money and reinvested these savings in money market funds and other money market investments with much higher yields. This disintermediation resulted in losses of $6.4 billion in deposits in 1981 and many billions more in 1982.

Depository institutions may issue certificates of deposits and other forms of time deposits (that is, not passbook accounts) which may be offered to the saver at market rates of interest (see Table 6.2). Forced to resort to such certificate financing, thrifts have been able to recapture some of the lost savings, but at frightful losses in terms of earnings. In effect, thrifts have been lending long at an average yield of about 8 percent and borrowing short at above 10 percent, resulting in losses.

The only hope for thrifts is that interest rates decline as they were beginning to do in the second half of 1982, and that they can improve the earnings on their mortgage holdings as old mortgages are paid off. The yields on mortgage investments should improve as

TABLE 6.2
The Changing Deposit Mix at Savings and Loans
(percentage distribution)

Year	NOW and Passbook	Fixed Rate Certificate and Special Accounts	Market Rate CDs
1966 (10/31)	88.3	11.7	—
1970	59.4	40.6	—
1971	54.6	45.4	—
1972	50.6	49.4	—
1973	46.7	53.3	—
1974	44.1	55.9	—
1975	42.7	57.3	—
1976	40.3	57.6	2.1
1977	37.9	59.7	2.4
1978	31.9	57.0	11.1
1979	25.3	41.0	33.7
1980	21.0	24.2	54.8
1981 (prel.)	19.4	13.0	67.6
1982 (est.)	20.8	8.6	70.6

Source: "1982 Savings and Loan Sourcebook," United States League of Savings Institutions, as updated by author.

"due on sale" clauses in existing mortgages are paid off when individuals sell their homes. The new legislation passed in 1982 overturns any state laws which banned "due on sale" clauses. This change should speed up the turnover of mortgages, permitting thrifts to improve their returns by writing many more new mortgages at rates averaging above 10 percent than they could have previously when many states banned the practice of calling in mortgages when a house sale occurred.

Thus the Regulation Q ceiling has caused thrifts to lose passbook accounts to higher yielding money market funds on the one hand and to higher yielding certificates of deposits issued by commercial banks and thrifts (out of necessity) on the other hand.

The result is massive savings outflows which in some months of 1982 reached $4 billion a month. Many thrifts have been forced to merge to prevent insolvency. The Federal Deposit Insurance Corporation calculates that about 1,000 thrifts are in danger of becoming insolvent. Forced marriages with stronger thrifts prevent depositor inconvenience and delay in receiving funds.

Despite the disparity between Regulation Q ceilings and open market rates, passbook deposit accounts still represent a large item on the liability side of thrift institutions' balance sheets. Despite the appeal of the higher rate from money market funds and certificates of deposit, passbook accounts still constitute over 20 percent of savings and loans' deposit liabilities. This reflects the basic resistance to change on the part of the consumer. This lethargy protects the thrifts from massive runs which would swamp the system.

The banking legislation, passed in October of 1982, permits thrifts and commercial banks to offer a new liquid asset account which will be fully equivalent to money market funds. Since these new accounts will bear deposit insurance, they may be more attractive to investors than money market funds. However, many thrift officials fear they will "cannibalize" existing passbook savings accounts which to date have remained the mainstay of the thrifts. They fear that the lethargy that has been prevalent so far will dissolve as passbook account savers realize they can gain higher interest rates with no penalties or risk by transferring over to liquid asset accounts from passbook accounts. Some thrifts feel that the liquid asset accounts should have had a higher minimum than the $2,500 minimum finally determined by the Depository Institutions Deregulation Committee to discourage this threat of cannibalization.

The new accounts will be appealing to the consumer. Thrift officials point out that the new liquid asset account will have the "built-in" advantages depositors at thrift institutions have always enjoyed. Depositors, for example, will not be dealing with "disembodied" telephone voices only interested in discussing rates of return. At savings institutions the customer deals with real, live people offering a variety of other financial services including, notably, the preferred availability of mortgage credit to savings depositors. Furthermore, most savings accounts of the passbook type have balances of less than the $2,500 required for liquid asset accounts and in that sense they are locked in to the lower yielding passbook accounts. Finally, savings officials point out that Regulation Q is scheduled to be phased out over a six year period, and not later than 1986. This schedule can be accelerated by the Depository Institutions Deregulation Committee and indeed they have already removed controls on the penalty provisions of some certificates of deposit.

Many of the mergers arranged by the federal regulatory authorities involve interstate marriages. It is difficult to find healthy thrifts willing to take on failing concerns. Many of these mergers, therefore, reflect a different motive, that is, the desire of commercial banks and thrift institutions to enter the interstate market on the heels of a takeover of an ailing thrift.

Examples of mergers with a dual motive include Citibank's takeover of an ailing San Francisco thrift institution and the nationwide combination of three ailing savings and loans associations to form First Nationwide.

PRODUCT STRATEGIES

Variable mortgages, which automatically increase or decrease the interest rate with the market rate, appear to be the long-term solution to the disintermediation problem of the thrifts. However, it will take years for this new format to work its way into the system. The average maturity of outstanding mortgages is approximately 10 to 12 years. In a landmark case the Supreme Court ruled unconstitutional any state law which bans the "due on sale" clause in existing mortgages of federally chartered associations. To further clarify the situation, Congress overturned any state law banning these cancellation clauses in the recently enacted Depository Institutions Act of 1982. This is a key development because the average American moves every seven years and if the resale of his house terminates an existing mortgage then the savings institutions will be able to refinance the purchase of the house with a new mortgage at market rates considerably higher than the rate on the old mortgage. Thus the recent court rulings, combined with the favorable legislative action, appear to constitute a major breakthrough in aid for thrifts by permitting them the opportunity to refinance mortgages at the higher yields now available in the open market.

Variable mortgages appear to be gaining in popularity. Last year, variable mortgages accounted for over 50 percent of the new mortgages written.

Variable mortgages come in three basic forms:

1) payment increases or decreases as interest rate goes up and down. The variable rate is usually tied to the interest rate on U.S. Treasury Bills or the prime rate.
2) mortgage payments are fixed but the term of the mortgage varies as the interest rate goes up or down. Portion of monthly payment for interest varies inversely with principal.
3) variations on the first two plans, including final "balloon" payments, share in the equity accumulated in the house, and "scaled-up" payments built into the mortgage repayment schedule.

Federal regulations are being liberalized to permit more variable mortgages. For example, in 1981, the Federal Home Loan Board approved a change in its rules which permits federally chartered savings and loan associations to write mortgages with adjustable interest rates pegged to an index but with no limit on how far and how often the rates could rise or fall.

Some credit experts forecast a demand for more than $2 trillion in new mortgage financing in this decade, an amount more than two times the total of mortgages outstanding at the end of 1980. With deregulation eliminating privileges enjoyed (or suffered) by the thrift industry under Regulation Q, housing will have to pay top dollar for this new money in the open market, assuming mortgage rates stay high over the rest of the decade.

Moreover, many experts in the housing field feel that the housing industry must find a better way to build a secondary market for mortgages in the future. This is necessary because of the growing involvement of individuals in financing the sale of homes with some form of purchase mortgage. In the 1970s individuals financed only 30 percent of U.S. residential mortgage debt while the balance, or 70 percent, of such loans came from financial entities. In the 1980s, so far, these percentages have been reversed, with individuals holding much more of the mortgage debt than previously. In order to accomodate this new source of home mortgage financing, the industry will have to improve the secondary market for mortgages. The secondary market is where the individual who holds a mortgage can liquidate that holding. Currently, the secondary market serves primarily the savings institutions and is not designed for individuals seeking to liquidate mortgage loan holdings. About the only outlet available to the individual mortgage holder is the local mortgage banker who acts as a sort of intermediary between the seller and the final investor, usually a thrift institution, or an institutional investor such as life insurance companies or pension funds. Behind the mortgage banker stands the Federal National Mortgage Association and the Government National Mortgage Association, but they essentially deal only with the savings institutions buying up unwanted existing mortgages and repackaging them into "participation" or "pass through" bond offerings issued by the federal agencies involved. What is needed is the creation of an active trading market with dealers making markets for outstanding mortgages in some fashion. The big problem is that each mortgage is a "unique" debt representing the credit standing and housing value backing that individual mortgage. Perhaps the federal agencies, working with the local mortgage brokers, could develop a "pass through" bond denominated in amounts as low as $1,000 which would be sold to individuals and actively traded in a secondary market similar to the trading market for corporate bonds. The federal agencies, of course, represented a step in this direction by purchasing mortgages from the thrifts and then repackaging them into "pass through" and "participation" bond offerings by the agencies themselves, but these bonds are purchased mainly by institutions and the secondary market in which they trade does not afford the individual holder of a mortgage instrument a means of selling his holding.

Thrifts are hoping that the recent broadening of the permitted lending areas for thrifts, included in the recent banking legislation, will enable them to shift to a broader form of lending not so dependent on mortgage loan financing. For example, thrifts can now make consumer loans up to 30 percent of assets and commercial loans up to 10 percent of their assets. This means that the required 80 percent minimum to be invested in housing loans has been reduced to 60 percent.

One area in which thrifts have been innovating is the development of new liability accounts. Thrifts developed the NOW account wherein interest is paid on checking accounts. The advantage of these accounts to the thrifts was that the interest paid fell under the Regulation Q or passbook account rates. Thus, by offering the checking account privilege, thrifts were able to maintain more low Regulation Q interest rate accounts, preserving a positive profit spread in relation to the interest thrifts made on the old mortgages in their investment portfolios. The NOW account format was authorized for all depository institutions in 1980 under the banking legislation enacted by Congress in that year.

In order, however, to meet the competition for new deposits from commercial bank certificates of deposits and from the money market mutual funds, thrifts have been forced in recent years to offer high yielding, market rate certificates and other time deposits, causing a sharp drop in earnings. This has forced many thrifts to seek mergers with other savings organizations which have sounder investment returns on their mortgage portfolios. Some thrifts were farsighted in selling out their lower yielding, older mortgages at slight losses before the huge jump in interest rates in recent years. These institutions reinvested these proceeds in new mortgages at higher current rates. In taking over "sick" thrifts, healthy thrifts have received discount inducements on the merger terms which make the transactions attractive.

Private Mortgages

As aforementioned, statistics show that private mortgages have been on the rise in recent years, accounting for over 50 percent of all new mortgages made in 1980. This results from the near bankruptcy of many thrifts and the extreme scarcity of new mortgage money from the thrift industry. Thus, the individual who wishes to sell his house under these conditions has had to take back some form of purchase mortgage as part of the home financing package to make the sale viable. These purchase mortgages involve many different variations but most of them fall under the general category of second mortgages. The overall financing package is usually arranged by the realtor, who describes the novel financing packages as "creative financing." This trend will probably reverse when interest rates come down or when the variable rate mortgage becomes more prevalent. In a move designed to help the private financing of home purchases, the Federal National Mortgage Association announced in late 1982 that it had extended its secondary mortgage purchase program to include purchases of second mortgages as well as first mortgages.

Thrifts will aggressively expand their new found consumer and commercial loan activities as authorized under the Depository Institutions Act of 1982. Consumer loans are typically for short terms of two to three years and thus are in step with the current earnings needs of the thrifts. However, the special nature of thrifts in housing finance will be damaged if they move too far away from home financing into the newly authorized areas of consumer loans and commercial loans. The recent federal legislation continues to require a minimum of 60 percent of assets in the home mortgage market and the broader lending powers to be phased in over a period of years. The new broader rules apply only to federally chartered thrifts, but this will probably force the individual states to adopt the broader lending powers. Most states still require that savings and loans associations invest a minimum of 80 percent of assets in home mortgages.

A variation of the certificate of deposit was authorized by Congress in 1981. These certificates, called "All Saver" certificates received considerable publicity, but did not gain much in the way of assets for the thrifts. Sales of the certificates totalled about $50 billion, but commercial banks sold much more of the new certificates than the thrifts did, possibly because the tax-free income feature appealed more to the typical higher income commercial bank account holder than to the lower income holder of a thrift account. Moreover, the new certificates' yields were calculated at three-quarters of the rate on U.S. Treasury Bills, which placed them below the comparable rates on taxable certificates. The authority to issue these certificates ran out at the end of 1981. The "All Saver" certificate did not solve the basic problem of disintermediation of the thrifts, they were essentially a stop-gap program—a "band aid"—to tide the thrifts over to a hopefully more viable interest rate environment.

Stock Brokerage Services

Thrift institutions are not prohibited from providing brokerage services and since late 1982, they have been marketing them—in much the same fashion as they introduced low cost life insurance. In one version, Security Pacific National Bank of California opened about 8,200 brokerage accounts serviced through the discount brokerage unit of the Fidelity Group. Volume so far is tiny, amounting to only 100 trades a day, but the trades are profitable even on the small volume. Eventually, Security Pacific plans to run its own brokerage subsidiary when volume permits. The Fidelity brokerage unit meantime has contracted to supply brokerage service for nine other banks and thrift institutions, and hopes to set up arrangements with 40 more thrifts.

A new brokerage unit, Invest, a subsidiary jointly-owned by several thrifts, began offering services on a membership basis to the more than 4,000 savings institutions in the nation. The foray into the securities business comes with the consent of the Federal Home Loan Bank Board, which gave its approval in early 1982 to the founding partners of the new group. The plan, however, has drawn mixed reviews from analysts who question whether thrift institutions, many of which continue to suffer big outflows of deposits while continuing to be saddled with low yielding mortgages, should be getting into another interest sensitive business. There is also widespread suspicion that the typical savings and loan depositor—conservative, safety conscious and not particularly affluent—is not the sort to dabble in the stock market. Donald Crawford, senior vice president of the Securities Industry Association, a trade group opposed to the plan, questioned whether the typical customer of a savings and loan association buys and sells securities, and if he does, he is probably not the type of "upscale" customer that the large commercial broker/dealers are used to working with. But, the promoters of the new idea said that they expected to have 8,000 registered representatives working on securities transactions for thrift customers. Since these brokers will be working for a salary, rather than commissions, they will be discouraged from "hustling" customers to buy and sell stocks. This feature, the promoters believe, will make the new brokerage service particularly attractive to customers who may be wary of stocks. By eliminating the commission incentive, the promoters claim that they have eliminated the major conflict of interest in the securities business.

Most analysts continue to be skeptical of the plan. One questioned whether diversifying into the brokerage industry made sense in the long run since thrifts are at that phase of the economic cycle (late 1982) where funding mortgages is likely to be quite profitable over the next several years. Another analyst commented that "stocks are sold, they're not bought—it's like life insurance, and you need highly motivated sales persons to develop volume—the approach won't work with non-commission sales people who don't generate ideas."[1]

PRICE STRATEGIES

Interest cost varies widely but the key factor is the spread between the cost of money to the thrift and the effective lending rate that the thrift can obtain in the mortgage and loan markets. This spread traditionally has hovered between one-half of 1 percent to 1 percent but has been negative for some time because of the nature of the thrifts' assets and liabilities. The thrust of the variable rate debt instrument is to eliminate this disparity of rates between long-term assets and short-term liabilities typical of the financial service industry.

PLACE STRATEGIES

As with the other banking institutions in the financial service industry, thrifts control their outlets. This gives them the opportunity to test-market new ideas at selected branches at relatively low cost and delay. Unlike the commercial banks, savings and loan holding companies have been able to branch out into the interstate markets. Savings and loan regulators have already permitted interstate mergers of ailing thrifts. Financial experts believe that the continued weakness of the thrift industry will force the regulators to allow more mergers of healthy thrifts across state lines.

PROMOTION STRATEGIES

Advertising and sales promotion techniques are used extensively in the thrift industry to promote the acquisition of new accounts. Sales promotion approaches include gifts for opening new accounts or introducing new accounts to the thrift organization. Advertising tends to feature products offered, convenience, and safety. Thrifts have not adopted a "personal banker" approach; rather they rely on sales specialists in individual product areas. Sales people are assigned to sections of the bank to answer inquiries and open new accounts. Thus, there is an officer available to discuss life insurance and IRAs, as well as specialists who handle inquiries on home mortgages, consumer loans, and special deposit plans. The sales people are salaried with some bonuses offered as an incentive to production. Promotional programs are handled by marketing staff people who coordinate the thrift's promotional campaigns and act as liasons between the advertising agency and top management.

NOTE

1. "Thrift Units Beginning to Offer Stock Services," *The New York Times*, November 8, 1982.

SEVEN

The Insurance Industry

THE STRUCTURE OF THE INDUSTRY

The insurance industry consists of mutual and stock companies. Mutual companies, which are owned by the policy holders, include the old line giants of the business such as Metropolitan, Prudential, Equitable, and New York Life, most of which are New York companies. Stock companies comprise the balance including Travelers, Aetna, CIGNA and Hartford. These companies are primarily property and casualty companies with many located out of New York State (see Tables 7.1 and 7.2).

Benefit payments for the life insurance industry run about $49 billion a year but are not predictable for the casualty companies. New premiums paid by policy holders run about $80 billion for both life insurance companies and casualty companies.

Technology, specifically the computer, has been synonymous with the industry's progress and profits, enabling them to make substantial cost reductions and facilitating new product introductions. State regulations govern the industry—insurance companies remain the only financial service sector which has evaded federal regulation. Federal law respects and recognizes the primacy of state law in the regulation of the insurance industry. This grows out of the industry's self regulation of unfair practices

TABLE 7.1
The Ten Largest Life Insurance Companies
(in billions of dollars)

	1981 Assets
Prudential Insurance	$ 62.5
Metropolitan Insurance	51.7
Equitable Insurance	36.7
Aetna Life & Casualty	25.1
New York Life Insurance	21.1
John Hancock Insurance	19.9
Connecticut General	15.1
Travelers Insurance	14.8
Northwestern Mutual	12.1
Massachusetts Mutual	10.0

Source: Best's Review, July 1982, A. M. Best Co.

TABLE 7.2
The Ten Largest Property and Casualty Insurance Companies
(in billions of dollars)

	1981 Assets
Travelers Insurance	14.8
Allstate Insurance	8.6
Aetna Insurance	7.0
Travelers Indemnity	5.2
United States F & G	4.2
Aetna Life & Casualty	4.0
INA	3.7
State Farm	3.6
St. Paul Fire & Marine	3.5
Hartford Insurance	3.5

Source: Bests' Key Rating Guide, 1982 edition, A. M. Best Co.

under state laws and oversight that, in turn, resulted from the findings of the Armstrong Commission in New York State and other state investigations conducted early in this century in the wake of widescale insurance industry scandals.

While many insurance companies operate in all states a larger number operate on a regional basis, primarily to avoid meeting the requirements of New York State's insurance regulations. The national companies include those which have qualified to do business under New York State's tough insurance law, the most restrictive of any state insurance law. New York State law stipulates that to qualify to do business in New York State, an insurance company must observe the New York State requirements in all other states. Thus New York State law becomes effectively the national law for all companies wishing to do business in all states. Among other requirements, New York State limits stock investments for life insurance companies to 10 percent of assets, restricts commissions on whole life policies to 55 percent of the first year premium and limits commissions for both term and whole life policies to 15 percent of premiums after the first year (including the first year for term policies). Regional companies (those that do not wish to meet New York's regulations) operate outside New York State, and typically pay first year commissions of two to three times the level permitted in New York. However, national companies can bypass New York State law by setting up affiliates but this is very expensive and has been resorted to by only a handful of companies.

TRENDS

In the life insurance field, term and group insurance have replaced whole life as the biggest sellers (see Table 7.3). Direct sellers are taking business away from independent agents especially in the property and casualty business. A basic principle persists that life insurance—essentially an unwanted product—must be sold, whereas casualty and property insurance is essential and the consumer, therefore, shops around for the best deal when in the market for automobile or homeowner insurance coverage.

Inflation has impacted the life insurance company picture. A

TABLE 7.3
Distribution of Life Insurance by Major Type
(in billions of dollars)

Year	Whole Life Including Endowment	Term	Credit	Group
1975	100.8	91.7	49.0	94.6
1976	113.1	106.8	63.7	104.7
1977	125.1	128.1	75.3	116.1
1978	140.1	150.5	94.1	124.2
1979	153.9	184.2	99.8	156.5
1980	172.8	222.5	87.2	183.2
1981	247.7	248.7	89.6	278.8

Note: Amounts shown represent the face value of new coverage written in the years shown.

Source: Best's Review, A. M. Best Co.

steadily eroding dollar means the typical breadwinner must own about $45,000 worth of life insurance in 1981 to provide the same level of real coverage as $31,200 in coverage would have provided five years earlier and $22,800 in coverage, ten years ago. Employers who provide group coverage have been forced to increase life insurance coverage in line with higher pay scales.

As a result of more women working female buyers of life insurance comprised about one-fifth of all new life policies issued in 1981. Young people buying insurance for the first time tend to purchase term rather than whole life.

Life insurance premiums, reflecting competition, have been decreasing steadily counter to the trend in the cost of living. Declining mortality rates aid this trend.

The Federal Trade Commission issued a 455 page staff study in 1980 that found that policy holders were losing billions of dollars a year because of the poor rate of return—only 1.3 percent—on the savings component of whole life policies. The conclusion of the Federal Trade Commission study was that policy holders would do better to buy term and invest their premium savings in the money market. These findings were rebutted by the industry. The National Association of Life Underwriters distributed several hundred thousand pamphlets with a point-by-point rebuttal. On the cover of their pamphlet, in red ink, appears the legend "Warning: the National Association of Life Underwriters has determined that the Federal Trade Commission is dangerous to your life insurance." The upshot was that the Senate moved to restrict the Federal Trade Commission's authority to investigate the insurance business, which is regulated by the individual states under the McCarran-Ferguson Act of 1945.

Nonetheless, policy loans are increasing, causing insurance companies to raise loan rates on new policies written and/or introduce variable policy loan rates pegged to the prime rate or some other benchmark. Policy loans, currently about $53 billion, could jump to $160 billion or 90 percent of reserves.

According to a study published in *Best's Review* in 1981 new individual life insurance policies are proliferating to meet the needs of an inflationary economy, including:

Non smoker premium	Variable life
Indeterminate premium plans	Adjustable life
Modified whole life	Universal life

Independent life insurance agents, who used to handle half of the insurance business, are in trouble. Commissions per agent employee declined to $42,760 in 1980 for the second year in a row, down from $44,350 down from the year before. Agents have declined in number to 67,000 from 85,000 in 1970. Part of this reflects falling commissions in a "soft" market but the primary reason is the assault of direct writers on independent agents. Direct writers, such as Allstate and State Farm, have increased their market share to 57 percent versus 36 percent for the independents. Direct writers are particularly effective in property and casualty business, less so in life insurance underwriting. Merrill Lynch is packaging a franchising approach to help independent agents against the big brokers. Direct writers are extending their operations into commercial lines. Large brokers are absorbing independent agents.

Property and casualty insurance differs from life insurance, since casualty losses are not as predictable as death claims. Profits therefore fluctuate widely, based on underwriting experience. The favorable investment returns of property and casualty companies have in most years offset unfavorable underwriting experience. State Farm and Allstate have pioneered direct selling, emphasizing lower premiums in home and automobile lines. People and businesses must have property and casualty insurance and they gravitate to the most economical policy.

Life insurance companies are diversifying into the property and casualty field, usually by merger. Another trend has been diversification into the securities field. Earlier, INA bought a 25 percent interest in Paine Webber. CIGNA, which was created by merger of INA with Connecticut General, in a counter trend has spun off Paine Webber in a complicated securities transaction. One explanation for the step out of the securities business may be the reservations of Ralph Saul, CIGNA's chairman, based on the securities businesses' highly volatile performance in the past. Prudential, the nation's largest insurance company, bought control in 1981 of Bache, Halsey, Stuart, Shields, Inc. for $387 million. Some experts believe that there is not much synergy between stock brokers and insurers; Ralph Saul, chairman of CIGNA maintains, for example, that the insurance and brokerage businesses are quite different. "Stockbrokers tend to be more entreprenurial and protective of their lists of clients than an insurance salesman."

TABLE 7.4
Growth of the Life and Property and Casualty Insurance (in billions of dollars)

Year	Life Insurance Company Assets	Property/Casualty Company Assets
1965	158.9	41.8
1970	207.3	58.0
1975	289.3	93.3
1980	500.0	150.0

Source: Best's Review, A. M. Best Co.

Dean Witter worries about the effect of risk averse management attitudes of insurance companies on Wall Street.[1]

PRODUCT STRATEGIES

Term and group policies are growing in the life insurance field while whole life is declining. Universal life which invests reserves in higher yielding investments than with conventional whole life is an attempt to turn around the whole life concept. The savings component has declined drastically as disintermediation through policy loans has reached epic proportions. Variable life is another new product coming into vogue to create a cash value type of policy with new inflation-hedged features and more aggressive investment policy.

Insurance companies, along with commercial banks, mutual fund management companies, investment counseling firms, and New York Stock Exchange firms constitute the major financial service companies competing for the highly lucrative pension management business. Life companies have tailored two products especially for pension plan funding. The first group consists of deferred annuities used to fund defined benefit pension plans which call for a fixed commitment by a company to pay a certain benefit to a retiring employee and his spouse for life. The benefit usually relates the retiring employee's career earnings to some payout formula, for example, one half of the last year's earnings or $10 per month for each year of service or some combination. Thus, insurance company actuaries project the size of the company's contribution to fund a plan to meet the future obligation, taking into account the ages, salaries, and years to retirement of the present employee group. Such plans must be reviewed by the actuaries every third year to make sure that investment performance has equaled or exceeded the actuarial assumption and to make adjustments in the employee population and earnings. About 30 percent of all pensions fall in this group and life insurance companies tend to dominate this business in contrast to banks, mutual funds, and New York Stock Exchange investment advisory firms.

The other type of pension plan, called a defined contribution plan requires a set contribution, usually a fixed percentage of payroll, into a plan for which the insurance company provides investment management services. These plans are segregated from the other assets of the life insurance company in so-called separate accounts. Insurance companies have not acquired much of this business due to poor investment performance and a negative perception on the part of pension fund managers of insurance companies as being too overly cautious and conservative to manage such accounts effectively.

New Product Strategies

According to Michael F. Cuscaden, a marketing vice president of Prudential, new product ideas come from four main sources:[2]

1) the field sales force
2) new legislation, for example, IRA accounts
3) competition from other life insurance companies
4) competition from other financial service firms such as banks and mutual funds.

Prudential first develops a consensus with the field sales force on a proposed new product. It then forms a task force to research new product ideas and develop a position paper in 90 to 120 days. The task force team then breaks up into subgroups to develop in-depth studies of each specific area, leading up to the final step, which is to target the launch date and price.

Other companies concentrate more intensively on the upper income market. This market is growing and needs help on estate and income tax problems.

Another route followed by some companies is to add products that give agents a major source of additional commissions, for example additional products in the auto and homeowners insurance area. These are demand products, the need for which is easily recognized by the client.

Yet another observer feels that new products will be based on new money rates. At the same time there will be a greater trend toward unbundling of protection, accumulation, and retirement features. There is a need to offer mutual funds, money funds, and other savings devices in the life insurance field. Increased emphasis should be placed on sales of life cycle policies where protection varies with the life stage of the individual. At the same time, this observer feels the marketing system will change in the foreseeable future:

- lead time for new product development will decline
- commissions will change to stimulate more sales and to prevent agents from making a big killing by shooting for one or two big orders rather than steady production
- there will be more and better packaging of financial services. Long-term bonds and mortgages will undergo significant changes for the pension fund market including a rebirth of interest in immunization theory (protecting capital against fluctuation caused by interest volatility).

Meanwhile, one new product of the late 1970s, Universal Life, has really caught hold. Although Universal Life accounted for only 2 percent of new life insurance premiums in 1981, this increased to about 9 percent of premiums in 1982 and is expected to account for more than 20 percent of premiums in a few years. Only about 100 of the 11,500 life companies offer this new concept but this number should grow sharply after New York approves the policy, a development which is expected in the near future. At one point there was a question as to the treatment of the investment for tax purposes. In fact, Metropolitan and other large insurance companies thought that the IRS would rule against the tax-deferral features of the new policy. This was clarified by new federal legislation which provided temporary guidelines for the tax treatment until permanent regulations are issued (by January 1, 1984).

Universal life, which has been sold for about three years, separates the insurance and savings aspects of a policy, so that the portion of the premium not used for insurance protection is invested, typically in short-term securities that accrue tax-free interest. Policyholders can, within certain limits, raise and lower their premiums and yields are generally larger than those on whole life policies.

Whole life insurance is a permanent form of insurance that builds up cash values over the term of the policy and has level premiums, this contrasts with term insurance, which is pure protection only and does not build up any cash value.

PLACE STRATEGIES

Most insurers do not control outlets, relying instead on independent agents and brokers for distribution. Some have their own sales forces and a growing number are resorting to direct selling through advertising, supplementing the efforts of their direct sales force and bypassing altogether the independent agent system. There has also been a trend toward brokers acquiring insurers. This trend contains the seeds of conflict of interest. Insurance brokers are supposed to be independent, seeking the best possible insurance coverage for their clients at the lowest possible cost. Many question how an insurance broker can maintain his independent stance when the broker owns an insurance company.

In the field of direct mail, credit cards have greatly simplified direct selling. Additionally, a substantial portion of the annual premiums on life insurance sold by direct mail is billed directly to the credit card and payment is pre-authorized by the card holder, thus guaranteeing the automatic renewal of coverage when the policy comes up for renewal. Alternatively, the policy holder can authorize the bank to pay the insurance premium directly, thus saving the insured the bother and expense of writing and mailing checks.

In the profit sharing/pension plan area, the companies control the marketing through their corporate group departments. Their principal competition is the large brokerage concerns that tend to write very large group business by aggressively packaging the best possible coverage at the lowest price.

PRICE STRATEGIES

Premiums are dropping as competition intensifies. Most price concessions apply to whole life where premiums are the highest and most lucrative to the company. Premiums tend to be much lower on term and group policies and therefore afford less opportunity for price cutting. Group and term policies tend to have the smallest agent commissions as well, but since group contracts usually cover a large number of individuals, the commissions in aggregate on this business usually warrant a heavy sales effort on the part of the broker or the life insurance company's home office group department.

Management fees for investment management services for employee benefit plans are subject to negotiation and are competitive with those charged by commercial banks and large investment advisory firms.

PROMOTION STRATEGIES

Both life and casualty companies use heavy product and institutional advertising campaigns but the sales core of the business continues to rely on the independent and captive insurance agents. There is a growing trend, in promoting insurance, to the use of direct mail advertising featuring low rates and the convenience of billing by credit card. Over the years there has been constant friction between captive sales forces and the independent agent system. More recently, the mergers of insurance companies by giant brokers and acquisitions of agencies by life insurance companies have resulted in some integration of the selling channels. This trend makes the insurance business more consistent with other sectors of the financial service field that long have controlled their retail outlets of distribution.

Advertising has shifted from "doomsday" commercials to whimsical vignettes taking a light philosophical view of life and the liability of early death. Prudential, for example, has a series of commercials patterned after "Heaven Can Wait," a 1978 movie starring Warren Beatty. In a typical Prudential commercial, two angels in white three-piece suits fetch their customer, a healthy man far from his sunset years, at his weekly bowling match. As they escort him up an escalator to heaven, he protests "I thought I'd have more time." Replies one of the angels: "Doesn't everybody?" Prudential is the nation's largest life insurer, and its whimsical approach contrasts markedly with the industry's typical delicate treatment of death. Even the name of their product, insurance marketers say, is an euphemism—"death insurance" would be more accurate.

Independent life agents can make up to 140 percent commission on the first year premiums on new whole life policies if they sell outside of the restrictions of New York. The insurance companies count on the fact that most life insurance is maintained by the insured for many years and they will be able to make up for the front-end commissions paid to the agent to write the contract in subsequent years, when commissions normally run only 15 percent of annual premiums. In New York State, first year commissions on whole life are limited to 55 percent of premium and to 15 percent of renewal premiums in the second and subsequent years. The life companies pay a high first year commission on whole life because it is the most lucrative insurance from the point of view of the insurance company. Whole life policies create the large cash reserves that are vital to the insurance company in terms of realizing annual earnings from the investments of these cash reserves. Because of the desirability of whole life policies, competition for agent's selling efforts between companies is intense, leading to the very high first year commissions. The commissions in subsequent years, commonly referred to as "trail" or renewal commissions, belong to the agent in most cases and many agents build a retirement annuity based on the renewal commissions. Captive agents, those employed directly by the insurance companies, usually do not have a lifetime right to these renewal commissions. They cease once the agent has left the company. Increasingly, once independent agents have relinquished part of their independence by signing primary contracts with lead insurance companies. These contracts guarantee that the agent will write the great bulk of his insurance with the lead insurance company which in return offers to subsidize part of his office rent and other selling and overhead expenses as part of the bargain. These contracts are subject to a great deal of abuse, as one might imagine.

Giant brokers like Marsh & McLelland and Alexander & Alexander and others have emerged to dominate the independent agency business. These brokers typically court all of the large business organizations and shop ruthlessly for the best coverage at the lowest price for the insured. They have, in recent years, begun to absorb small insurance agents to strengthen their position in the dominant lines and in many specialty lines such as marine insurance. As giant insurance companies react adversely, brokers increasingly have attempted to acquire their own insurance companies to ensure adequate supply of coverage. One must question whether a broker's independent judgement is compromised when he owns his source of insurance. Thus the industry is becoming more and more vertically integrated.

NOTES

1. "As More Insurers and Brokers Get Together, Some Experts Wonder How Well They Mix," *Wall Street Journal*, May 28, 1981.

2. "Developing New Life Products," Michael F. Cuscaden, *Best's Review*, July 1979, pp. 71–74.

EIGHT

Mutual Funds

THE STRUCTURE OF THE INDUSTRY

Income products have replaced equity products as the staples of mutual fund management companies. Equity funds were historically the backbone of the business but today they represent only a 20 percent share versus 80 percent ten years ago. The negative overhang from the "go-go" years of the 1960s has tarbrushed the industry with a negative image. The shakeout in the industry following the "go-go" debacle was fierce, especially for the highly aggressive growth funds that were the products of the speculative stock market of the late 1960s. Even the bellwether funds saw their assets and sales plunge in the aftermath. In the sobering decade of the 1970s, more than 150 mutual funds either liquidated or merged with stronger funds.

Despite the apparent success achieved by those firms that branched out into money funds and turned to direct marketing to sell them, there remains a sector of the industry—some 50 percent of assets—that has steadfastly held to the old tradition of selling shares through salesmen. Firms such as Massachussetts Financial Services and Putnam and Kemper are betting that the equities market will someday return to favor and prove their strategy of using stock brokers far superior to telephone marketing. If there is a revival in the fortunes of the equity-based funds, a good deal of the credit belongs outside of the mutual fund industry. "ERISA has been the best friend the well-managed mutual fund ever had," says James D. Fullerton, senior vice president of Capital Research & Management Co., in Los Angeles. Fullerton says the search for the best by the investor planning for his retirement has led to mutual funds. "Before ERISA, banks and insurance companies had a lock on the pension fund business and nobody paid a whole lot of attention to what sort of results they were getting."[1]

The mutual fund industry in the 1980s seems in a far stronger position to respond to competitive threats than it was during the 1973-74 stock market plunge that severely wounded the industry.

The reason for this strength can be found in new marketing strategies the funds adopted in desperation just as the stock market soured. Prior to that, the industry's entire marketing approach involved various forms of the Wall Street hustle. In the 1960s, the "go-go" investment mentality that swept across the country pushed the stock-oriented mutual fund industry's total assets from $15.8 billion at the start of the decade to nearly $50 billion at the close. Yet even as the industry basked in resounding growth, the seeds of its destruction were being sown in the inevitable crash of stock prices in 1973-74, a stock decline as great as any save the great stock market crash of 1929. After the fall, mutual fund managers had to find a new vehicle to revive sales. Out of this search came money funds and the concept of a family of funds to provide a fund vehicle keyed to every investment need. Money funds were a major product breakthrough for this financial service sector. Along with the money funds, mutual fund management companies began to learn how to live without broker/dealer distribution. They found that they could market direct as effectively as they ever did through the broker/dealer. Moreover, the selling message could be controlled by the fund sponsor, not the broker representative whose sales pitch tends to exaggerate the prospects and create elevated expectations for performance that can not be satisfied.

Other major trends have been to develop pension fund management services for custom-tailored investment advisory services. Mutual fund management companies have taken a 19 percent share of pension fund management business largely at the expense of bank trust companies, insurance companies, and New York Stock Exchange investment adviser units. Mutual funds stress their equity management expertise based on the superior long-term record of the mutual funds. Some fund sponsors have developed niches in the emerging growth fields of the future such as technology, health care, energy, and automation. To complete their investment packages, some fund sponsors have also developed specialized income strategies such as bond immunization programs to offer to the pension fund market.

The new money market liquid asset accounts authorized for banks and savings institutions by the Depository Institutions Act of 1982 have forced mutual funds to fight back with new products and services of their own.

The consumer will benefit from the many new services that are being planned by mutual fund companies. New ideas include debit cards for making cash withdrawals from automated teller machines and "switch" advisories alerting investors in families of funds when to move into stocks and bonds and when to switch back again.

Within the next few years, the rapidly blurring distinctions among banks, mutual fund companies, and brokerage firms may disappear altogether. For example, two large mutual fund groups are expanding to offer a full range of financial services. Dreyfus Corp. is buying one New Jersey bank and has applied for a charter to start another bank in that state. Fidelity Group, which already has a discount brokerage unit, has received approval for a New Hampshire bank charter.

The launching of the new liquid asset accounts by the banks and thrifts should represent stiff competition for the investor/saver's dollar. Mutual fund companies believe the interest rates of the new bank accounts will be lower than money fund yields to cover financial institutions' higher "brick and mortar" costs. Some observers, however, predict that banks and thrifts will use the accounts as "loss leaders," matching or paying more than the money funds' rates to lure back some of the billions of dollars in deposits that money funds have siphoned off in recent years. Banks typically lend their assets out for longer periods than money funds and, accordingly, earn higher returns.

"No-load" direct distribution has largely replaced broker/dealer distribution. Broker/dealers in turn, have developed their own internally managed mutual fund products which are marketed by the broker/dealer salesmen. Broker/dealer distribution, however, continues to be important when a new fund idea is launched through an underwriting or when the fund concept is fairly sophisticated and intended to appeal to high-income investors with whom the broker has excellent contacts.

The elimination of most of the restrictions on mutual fund advertising, which previously banned the use of selling messages in paid advertising by the industry, has so far had only limited impact. Most advertising in recent years has promoted "no-load" mutual funds and in particular money funds, the most successful new product ever for the mutual fund industry. The Investment Company Institute, the mutual fund trade group, was able to force the Securities and Exchange Commission to eliminate the advertising restrictions because they violated the mutual fund's rights; citing recent court rulings that the first amendment provides freedom of speech protection for commercial advertisers as well as for the individual citizen. The SEC now guides mutual funds in what they can use in advertising to avoid violating the law of fraud and fulfilling the full disclosure requirements of the securities acts, but the SEC can not order these guidelines to be followed.

When equity investing returns to investor favor, mutual fund advertising will undoubtedly turn to common stock funds, an area where misrepresentation looms large. The mutual funds will undoubtedly advertise their better performance records and their efficiency for the small investor. In late 1982, with the stock market booming once again, the industry began to promote the equity funds in mutual fund advertising. For example, Fidelity Group headlined that its stellar performer, Magellan Fund, was "Number One Again in Five Year Performance." Other mutual fund groups, including Vanguard's Explorer Fund, have begun to extoll the virtues and values of their common stock growth funds.

It remains to be seen whether mutual funds will be statesmenlike in their new found world of advertising freedom. It took over 50 years to throw off the restrictions imposed on advertising. These restrictions grew out of the abuses of the 1920s when promises of investment performance by the closed-end trusts (the darlings of the bull market of the 1920s and the direct predecessors of the mutual fund of today) verged on outright fraud. It is hopefully significant that the fraudulent misrepresentations of the 1920s were largely based on "word-of-mouth" sales presentations, not paid advertisements by the closed-end trusts which generally followed a conservative tone. But Congress restricted the industry with rules enacted to curb the unbridled claims of the hucksters.

MARKETING EVOLUTION IN THE MUTUAL FUND INDUSTRY

Pre-1960—Mutual funds were primarily a single product, the common stock fund, sold exclusively by stock brokers. Some mutual funds were sold direct without sales charge but they constituted a very small portion of the total business. Advertising was not used and required the so-called "tombstone" format without any sales message. Although mutual funds constituted an important product for broker/dealers, they accounted for a very small share of total consumer savings.

Sales Period—This period roughly parallels the stock market boom years of the late 1960s dubbed by many as the "go-go" years. During this period, mutual fund sales swelled to record levels heavily oriented towards common stock funds, particularly the more aggressive growth funds. The distribution of mutual funds reached record proportions greater than the boom period of the closed-end trusts in the 1920s and the mutual fund's share of consumer savings doubled during this period. This period can also be characterized as the mass production/mass marketing period. Mutual funds were primarily common stock and growth-oriented; the family of funds concept and product segmentation were unheard of during this time. The sales message depended heavily on exciting the customer's desire (greed) for short-term profits and the broker's enthusiasm was buttressed by high commissions and enhanced by substantial brokerage reciprocal business practices, making mutual funds the most profitable single product to the broker/dealer.

Retrenchment and Product Innovation Era—The "soaring sixties" were followed by the "sober seventies." The stock market collapse of 1973-74 challenged that of the early 1930s in severity. The SEC began to look critically into the mutual fund distribution system. Reciprocal brokerage practices were substantially curbed and the SEC actively promoted the idea of "no-load" funds as a way of reducing the cost of mutual funds to investors. The public became disenchanted with common stocks. This was evidenced by falling sales of common stock mutual funds and the revelation by the New York Stock Exchange that over five million shareowners had departed the ranks of the nation's shareowners, a finding based on their periodic nose count of the shareowner population. Mutual fund companies were forced to innovate. New products were launched emphasing income objectives and safety features. The family of funds concept was born, offering free exchange privileges to permit investors to change their investment vehicle based on a different stage in the life cycle or concern with the market. This froth of new products culminated with the development of the money market funds in the early 1970s.

Changing Distribution Patterns—While product changes of the 1970s were highly visible, distribution changes were equally profound. Direct "no-load" distribution began to supplant broker/ dealer distribution. Broker/dealers countered by launching their own mutual funds, especially money funds which broker/dealers perfected into the cash management account. Advertising on a much wider scale, with liberalized rules began to appear to promote the direct distribution of "no-load" funds.

Full Service Concept—The proliferation of services and types of mutual funds with interfund exchange privileges have forced mutual fund companies to merge in order to be able to provide the minimum service required in the mutual fund business. Long-range planning has replaced the pragmatic approach of the past.

Market Development Period—Many mutual fund complexes have developed specialized money management divisions to tap the investment management business of the pension funds. This has brought mutual funds in direct competition with the commercial banks, insurance companies, and others in pursuit of this business.

PRODUCT STRATEGIES

Money funds are the stars of the mutual fund firmament. Other income fund products have also had some success, including bond funds, option funds, and tax-free funds. Packaging techniques are multiplying, usually combining life insurance with equities and bonds. Interfund exchange privileges allow investors to change their bond/stock ratio to adjust for changes in the economy and in the life cycle of individuals as they approach retirement. One variation of this approach is packaging several specialty funds featuring specific growth areas under a common umbrella. Fidelity Group is marketing such a combination called Fidelity Select Portfolios. The Fidelity bundle includes individual funds stressing investments in technology, health care, energy, precious metals, utilities, and financial services.

Mutual funds have developed the money funds to resemble bank-related products. Money funds also include checking account features, with the added benefit that the investor continues to earn interest on his money fund while the check clears through the banking system. In fact, the competition from money funds became so intense that banks tried (unsuccessfully) to force money funds to meet the deposit reserve requirements of the Federal Reserve. Failing that, the banks received authorization in the 1982 banking legislation to launch their own form of money funds, euphemistically called liquid asset accounts.

Many large brokerage firms have developed competitive money fund products with additional flexibility to access the customer's margin account, bank letter of credit, as well as interest payments, stock purchases, checking account privileges, credit cards and so on. Merrill Lynch's phenomenally successful Cash Management Account involves five separate services linked together by computer with the customer's money market fund. Merrill Lynch's service now has 900,000 clients with assets approaching $50 billion.

Mutual fund companies have expanded their services to include the lucrative pension fund management field. Starting in the early 1970s, mutual funds now manage some 19 percent of pension fund assets through their pension fund money management affiliates. Mutual funds have found it necessary to launch separate money management subsidiaries to compete for this business. This move was dictated by the widespread misconception among pension fund administrators that mutual funds had poor performance records and that mutual funds are for the small investor. This latter shibboleth is particularly irksome to mutual fund promoters who note that their performance is substantially better than the banks and insurance companies and there has been a growing trend by pension funds to use mutual fund shares directly in their investment portfolios despite the widespread misconceptions of many pension administrators. For example, pension fund holdings of mutual fund shares totaled $7.7 billion at the end of 1981, up 54 percent over the previous year. But this is a very small percent of the overall pension market which has total assets of over $400 billion. As aforementioned, the principal competitors for this business are the bank trust companies (which have over 50 percent of the market but are steadily losing assets due to poor performance), insurance companies and New York Stock Exchange investment advisory units. Financial consultants such as Frank Russell and Lowrie Associates constantly monitor the performance of the competing money management firms and constitute a major conduit for channeling investment management contracts between the pension funds and the money management field.

PRICE STRATEGIES

Until the 1970s mutual funds were primarily priced with an 8.5 percent commission paid out to the broker/dealer who secured the order. Almost all mutual funds were sold to the public through the broker/dealer network. The trend over the past ten years, however, has been to bypass the broker/dealer and to sell without any front-end sales charge, a process commonly referred to as "no-load" distribution. The costs of selling are absorbed by the fund management and deducted from the management fees that the managers are paid by stockholders for investing their assets. The SEC has issued a new rule which permits "no-load" funds to require that stockholders defray a portion of the sales cost in addition to the payment of fees for the investing of the assets of the fund. This is justified because the danger to the fund shareholder is that continuing redemptions in excess of sales could strip the fund of its ability to manage its assets, A healthy fund with sales exceeding redemptions is a prerequisite and the fund shareholder should bear some of the promotion costs, to ensure that the fund has a healthy growth of sales in excess of its redemptions.

A variation on the sales load has been packages of insurance and mutual funds in which the insurance company pays the broker a commission on the sale of the package, but the customer does not pay any commissions unless he redeems his shares early (usually within five years), in which case he pays a reverse sales charge, scaled to the number of years he has held the fund. This penalty on early withdrawals discourages redemptions and at the same time recaptures sales costs that have to be paid by someone. It also avoids dipping into the management fee to finance sales; management fees should be used to buy investment advice. The insurance company thus is assured that the front-end selling costs will be recouped either from future earnings or from the reverse sales commission on early redemptions. This pricing arrangement is very popular with deferred annuity contracts where the funding vehicle is a specialized mutual fund. Many experts believe this technique ultimately will be adopted in conventional mutual fund pricing arrangements.

"No-load" distribution now accounts for 100 percent of money funds sales and over 30 percent of stock funds with the likelihood that "no-load" distribution will eventually become the dominant format. "No-load" distribution has several disadvantages, including heavy and continuing overhead expenses, increased advertising expenses, and the lack of commission incentives to induce brokers to promote mutual fund distribution. Some also claim the lack of a personal sales representative could lead to unwise investments by the public in speculative and other risky mutual funds. Some fear that "no-load" distribution could lead to a revival of the "go-go" mutual fund fad of the late 1960s. Notwithstanding these concerns the SEC has attempted to foster "no-load" distribution. As mentioned previously, the SEC recently ruled that a mutual fund may use a portion of its assets to promote the sale of new shares. In a variation of this pricing approach, the direct seller, IDS, has applied to the SEC for permission to drop front-end commissions, it would replace these by rolling more expenses into management fees combined with a reverse sales load.

Management fees scale down from as much as 2 percent to one-tenth of 1 percent, depending on asset size. Management fees have been increasing lately because of rising costs and the aforementioned trend to finance new sales of fund shares by using part of the management fee for marketing expenses.

PLACE STRATEGIES

The mutual fund industry is unique in the financial service industry, they do not have extensive branch selling offices as do their competitors in the banking, insurance, and stock brokerage businesses. This grew out of the historical reliance on the independent broker/dealer for distribution. The mutual fund industry is now turning away from the traditional reliance on the broker/dealer to direct selling and the use of controlled sales forces such as those of IDS and those of the insurance industry who are selling mutual funds as part of an insurance/mutual fund package. The securities industry broker/dealer is now becoming a direct competitor of the original wholesale mutual fund sponsors with broker-managed money funds, deferred annuities, and common stock funds.

The most important part of the merger of the insurance companies and mutual funds that has occurred in the past several years is that mutual funds gain distribution outlets through thousands of life insurance agents who are looking for a better, more profitable and flexible product than whole life and that combines both insurance and mutual funds in one package offering as well the tax shelter of deferred annuities. The combination of "no-load" distribution and the reverse sales charge has particular appeal for insurance companies with large sales forces. More insurance and mutual fund mergers are inevitable given the strong mutual distribution advantages that accrue from this combination.

PROMOTION STRATEGIES

Personal selling has been, historically, the primary promotion vehicle for mutual funds. They were similar to life insurance in that they had to be sold and that meant primary reliance on personal salesmanship. The only advertising employed was direct mail solicitation because of the need to include a prospectus with each solicitation. Advertising was almost non-existent because of the "tombstone" advertising rules which forebade the use of selling arguments in mutual fund advertisements.

The SEC has liberalized these rules, in part due to recognition that the first amendment guarantees freedom of speech for commercial citizens as well as private citizens, and in part due to the deregulation sweeping through the financial service industry. The SEC has issued suggested guidelines for mutual fund advertising. These guidelines suggest that mutual funds may discuss in their print and broadcast advertisements any information contained in their prospectuses including their yields and past performance records. The former limitations of the "tombstone" advertisements are swept aside. This new advertising freedom applies to advertising carried in general circulation newspapers and magazines as well as radio and television commercials. The SEC in its announcement said that it believes mutual funds need additional advertising freedom because of increased competition from savings and loans, banks, and other financial services. Technically, mutual fund companies do not need to follow the SEC guidelines, but most in the industry would consider that foolhardy. Under the Investment Company Act of 1940 a mutual fund must receive SEC approval of its registration statement before it can begin selling new shares to investors. Since these registration statements must be resubmitted to the SEC annually for approval, the SEC has "life and death" power over any mutual fund which tries to challenge its authority.

With the liberalization of advertising rules and the decline in broker/dealer distribution it is likely that newspaper, radio, and television advertising will grow significantly in the future. This has already become evident in the promotion of "no-load" funds, especially money funds. Last year, for example, the Fidelity Group spent an estimated $3 to $5 million on advertising and that was before the full impact of the liberalized SEC advertising rules went into effect. As common stock funds become popular once again, advertising should become more dedicated to the promotion of equity vehicles and probably will expand. Many believe that the real test of the ability of mutual funds to advertise without misrepresentation will come when they turn the focus of their advertisements to promoting common stock funds. There is a feeling that inherent conflicts in promoting common stock funds preclude the ability to do so without misrepresentation. This is because the fundamental appeal has to be the promise of high returns which are about as unpredictable as Maine weather!

It is unlikely that advertising will entirely supplant personal selling in the distribution of mutual fund shares. The Fidelity Group, for example, one of the largest advertisers, has opened an investor information center in New York and intends to open additional offices in the near future to help in the distribution of that firm's mutual fund products.

Moreover, advertising costs continue to increase geometrically and mass media promotion must depend on mass volume to make it pay. The cost for a minute of prime time network television time has increased from $40,000 in 1970, to 60,000 in 1975, to 135,000 in 1980. Daytime television network commercial time increased to $25,000 per minute in 1980 from $12,000 in 1975 and $5,000 in 1970.

The continued importance of personal selling in the mutual fund field is reflected in the armies of insurance agents and telephone sales people employed by mutual fund complexes to field telephone inquiries and convert these inquiries into sales.

The industry's trade association, The Investment Company Institute, completed production of a new promotional film, "Future Funds," for use in promoting the mutual fund concept before investor groups.

NOTE

1. "Mutual Funds Resurge," *Business Week*, March 31, 1980, pp. 70–1.

NINE

Pension Fund Management

Four major financial service giants are fighting vigorously for the dominant share of the nation's $400 billion pension fund business. These include the trust departments of commercial banks, investment advisory divisions of stock brokerage firms, mutual fund management companies, and insurance companies. The stakes are high, with management fees running about $1 billion a year.

Historically, commercial banks have been the dominant factor in this business with insurance companies far behind. It was very proper for a corporate financial officer to favor the bank as the steward of the company's pension fund. The bank was after all, the company's primary source of loans and, furthermore, who could criticize management for placing the stewardship of the pension fund with the trust affiliate of the bank?

Bank trust companies are highly regulated by the states and the federal government. The covenants of bank trust charters protect trust accounts from the vagaries of individual trustees and money managers, and for this reason pension fund administrators have long favored bank trust companies as the managers of the corporate pension fund pool.

All of this was changed by the Employee Retirement Insurance Act (ERISA) enacted by Congress in 1974. Among other things, ERISA requires pension fund trustees to seek out the best performing money manager to tend to the fund's assets and makes it a criminal offense for failure to provide the proper diligence in its oversight. This has meant annual reviews of performance of the fund's managers versus all other managers. To provide this service, specialized consulting firms have emerged which monitor investment performance of the money management field and provide this data to trustees for an annual consulting fee. They also visit and evaluate money managers for pension trustees, again for a fee. The average pension fund account now turns over from one manager to the next once every three to five years as a result.

As a result of this Congressional mandate for investment diligence, banks lost their predominant share of the pension fund management business. Mutual fund management companies, insurance companies, New York Stock Exchange firms and other independent investment advisory units have gained market share due to their superior investment performance record as recorded by the independent statistical agencies.

Richard A. Cantor, a former vice president of Chase Manhattan Bank's $4 billion investment advisory division, writing in *Institutional Investor* magazine, enumerated the reasons why banks have trouble managing investment accounts:[1]

1) Banks manage too much money to perform well.
2) Banks are wedded to archaic decision-making procedures.
3) Bank pay cannot hold good people.
4) Bank fees do not reflect investor realities. They are too low and not structured properly.
5) Banks play football with accounts, switching accounts and personnel too often.
6) Banks take all comers. They should specialize more.
7) Banks let administrative detail smother investment men.

Thus, ERISA opened up the pension fund management field to competition because of the redefinition of the "prudent man" rule requiring trustees to seek out the best performing money managers to enhance the fund's performance.

PRODUCT STRATEGIES

Many combination products have been developed. These have been divided into two broad categories generally referred to as passive and active management strategies.

Passive Strategies

Broad tactics have been developed including bond strategies that seek to provide a reasonably high income but at the same time immunize the bond portfolio against the wide fluctuations in the bond market. Bond markets have become extremely volatile in the past ten years, with widely fluctuating interest rates gyrating in tandem with equally wide swings in the rate of inflation. Other bond strategies emphasize spacing out maturities to hedge against secular changes in the yield curve and bond index funds that attempt to provide diversification among higher and lower quality bonds. Stock funds that mirror the broad stock averages commonly referred to as index funds are another broad category of passive funds. Under the widely followed modern portfolio theory, it is felt that the securities markets are so efficient that money managers can not outperform the market. As a result, index funds, which replicate the market as a whole, have grown in popularity with pension funds. Index funds are structured with no management fee other than an administration fee for maintaining the portfolio.

Active Strategies

At the other extreme are money managers who believe the market is not efficient and that expert money managers can outperform the broad market indexes. These active managers usually receive a fee two to three times greater than the passive managers. Active strategies tend to emphasize investment management in the dynamic areas of the market such as high technology, energy, health care, natural resource companies, and turnaround situations. The venture capital field is another in which pension funds have a growing interest. Active managers tend to emphasize specialties in their portfolio approach, some concentrating on small growth companies, others on areas in the emerging technology sectors and still others emphasizing technical analysis. Pension fund trustees prefer to select several managers with different investment styles to provide diversification of management as well as investment diversification.

PRICE STRATEGIES

Management fees sometimes are supplemented with fees for transactions and other activity charges, this is especially true in the bank trust companies. Management fees usually run one-quarter of 1 percent for accounts up to $5 to $10 million, becoming negotiated fees for assets in excess of this amount. As has been mentioned, passive managers' fees are much lower than active money managers. Brokerage commissions usually are placed by the manager with brokers who provide services to the manager, although frequently the pension fund trustees will designate certain brokers to receive commissions in return for services to the trustees. These include, notably, the services of stock brokers who monitor and report to the trustees on investment performance. Even though institutional brokerage rates are far lower than those paid by the small investor, the brokerage costs of institutions accounts for over 50 percent of all commissions generated currently on the New York Stock Exchange.

PLACE STRATEGIES

Distribution tends to be direct from the money manager to the pension fund, using sales executives or portfolio managers for the sales presentation. There exists much marketing debate as to whether the most effective presentation and sales coverage is obtained through the securities analysts who actually manage the securities portfolio or through professional sales representatives with investment training but who do not have portfolio responsibility. Advocates of the securities analyst doubling as the sales representative claim that the pension fund trustees want to be in touch with the people who are actually managing the account and not "some slick sales type." They also claim that client contact acts as a stimulant to better performance for the analyst and serves to keep the analyst aware of the changing objectives of the pension fund. Opponents claim that using the securities analyst as a sales representative dilutes the portfolio management and is counter-productive because the securities analyst is frequently not aware of the needs and desires of the pension trustee, leading to hostility and account switching. In other words, a professional investment sales representative can maintain account liaison more effectively than a portfolio manager whose job should be managing the portfolio. This school suggests that the portfolio manager is best used when investment results are reviewed with the client at the formal meetings with the full group of pension trustees, while a sales representative maintains contact on a regular basis in the interim. It is clear that there is no definite direction in this controversy. As one expert puts it, "pension management is a dual service, one part portfolio management and one part relationship management. The relationship portion is becoming increasingly important, so it's not surprising to see many money managers going in different directions."[2]

New account solicitation can also result from the activities of the aforementioned broker/consultants who specialize in moni-toring and evaluating the performance capabilities of money managers. They, of course, receive compensation which can be in the form of finders fees paid by the pension fund of one-half of 1 percent or in form of reciprocal brokerage commissions designated by the pension fund trustees on behalf of his services.

Role of the "Gatekeepers"

The key to new account solicitation in the pension field is the "gatekeeper." This corporate employee, usually from the corporate finance department, is charged with meeting with the repre-sentatives of money managers and maintaining files for the trustees on prospective new managers. The gatekeeper makes recom-mendations to the pension committee and, therefore, it is strate-gically important for potential money managers to maintain close and continuous contact with the gatekeeper if they hope to be included in periodic competitions for new money manager selection. On average, major pension managers are evaluated every three to five years and, therefore, it is important to have established an on-going relationship with the gatekeeper during the interim period leading up to a major re-evaluation.

There are a number of specialized firms that monitor investment results and evaluate competitive money managers for pension fund trustees. These firms include:

Lipper Analytical Services   Meeder & Associates
Amivest Corporation   J. H. Ayres & Co.
Investment Timing Service   Lowry Management Corporation

PROMOTION STRATEGIES

Some advertising is used in specialized pension magazines with an emphasis on performance comparisons. Publications that attract this type of advertising include *Pension and Investment News, Trusts and Estates, Institutional Investor* and the *Wall Street Journal.* The personal sales representation, however, as discussed above, remains the primary promotional strategy in the pension fund management business.

NOTE

1. "Why Banks Have Trouble Managing Investment Accounts," Richard A. Cantor, *Institutional Investor*, September 1968.

2. "Should Portfolio Managers Do Marketing?" Charles Ellis, *Institutional Investor*, June 1981.

TEN

Securities Firms

THE STRUCTURE OF THE INDUSTRY

The age of marketing is upon the securities industry. More and more firms are recognizing that there is a need to structure their business strategy to identify and satisfy the needs and wants of customers. Product planning, packaging, pricing, promotion, distribution, and servicing are increasingly being addressed from the customer's point of view.

More and more, the principal financial competitors of most securities firms are leading banks and insurance companies, rather than securities firms per se.

For years, one stop financial shopping was thought to be just around the corner, but instead a more evolutionary change is likely in the area of financial packaging. Every major financial service field has expanded its products and services, permitting customers to use fewer financial services companies. Attitude surveys indicate that many investors prefer to deal with fewer financial service suppliers. A clear need exists for repackaging services in more convenient bundles.

Financial planning could be a major service area that truly embraces the marketing concept. The industry is just starting to tap a new mass market, for example, the high income/low cash market (that is individuals with high current earnings who have not accumulated much financial or real assets. Inflation and other forces are pushing people into income brackets which formerly would have indicated a prime brokerage account, but because of high taxes, housing costs and educational expenses, needs to be channeled into tax-deferred accounts such as IRA and Keogh plans. This market has been barely scratched in terms of the securities industry. To tap this market, the industry needs to develop regular savings plans to build financial assets.

Regional firms are losing ground to national firms as the industry becomes more concentrated. The question remains whether the consolidation trend, in causing the disappearance of many regional firms, threatens the ability of the nation's smaller companies to go public and attract market makers in their stocks, and whether it impedes in any way the efforts of these companies to raise capital. One investment banker who is concerned about whether consolidation of regional firms into the "wire" houses threatens the nation's capital raising ability is Robert H. B. Baldwin, president of Morgan Stanley, a company that has relied heavily on regional firms to distribute securities of the underwritings it heads. His contention is that the local firm will do a superior job of selling a local issue because they know the local firm intimately and have a dedication to seeing the financing succeed.

The original concept of the securities concern as a reflection of an individual "star" analyst is rapidly being replaced with "General Motors" type management committees. It has been said that Charles Merrill would have far more difficulty starting up a firm today than he did in 1940. Despite this, specialty houses continue to thrive on Wall Street as institutional investors demand specialized services in rapidly emerging growth fields.

The 25 largest firms in the securities industry have increased their market share from 47.8 percent of the business in 1973 to 76.6 percent in 1982 (see Table 10.1).

The securities industry has very broad categories of firms including the department stores such as Merrill Lynch, Paine Webber and Shearson/American Express; the "Gucci's" such as Lehman and Donaldson, Lufkin and Janerette; the specialty houses such as Oppenheimer and Eberstadt; the surviving regional firms

TABLE 10.1
Market Share of Biggest Securities
Concerns*
(based on percent of
gross revenue)

Year	Top 25 Firms	Top 10 Firms
1973	47.8	33.6
1974	56.0	38.2
1975	58.1	40.1
1976	60.3	41.6
1977	62.4	41.4
1978	70.7	44.5
1979	70.1	48.4
1980	72.3	52.8
1981	74.4	55.5
1982 (9 mos.)	76.6	58.6

*The business mix of the largest firms contains substantial amounts of interest income which tends to inflate market share; it would be lower if market share were based on commissions alone

Source: "Securities Industry Trends," Securities Industry Association, 8(6), November 2, 1982.

such as Piper, Jaffray, and Rotan Mosle; the discounters such as Schwab and the outsiders—nonmember firms who deal in listed stocks off the board. The upheavals of the business have created opportunities for small specialty houses to fill the void left by the big firms. These small firms specialize in consulting services such as economic forecasting, options, leveraged buyouts, venture capital deals, and emerging growth company research. The very proliferation of services makes it difficult for even in-house brokers to keep up. One of the big firms, Merrill Lynch in an effort to solve this problem, is trying out a new system in a few of its branches featuring a "customer service representative" somewhat akin to the personal banker in commercial banking.

PRODUCT STRATEGIES

The proliferation of new products continues in the industry. Money funds, insurance and annuities, investment advisory services, option trading, cash management accounts, and IRA and Keogh plans are just a few of the areas introduced by stock exchange firms to smooth out the traditional cyclical earnings patterns of the stock brokerage business.

New ideas that have been introduced in recent years include commodity funds or pools which permit investors to participate in highly active and potentially profitable commodity and futures trading through the mutual fund vehicle managed generally by stock exchange firms.

Merrill Lynch started offering its cash management account five years ago and while more than a dozen competitors now have similar services on the market Merrill Lynch dominates the business with about 900,000 of the estimated 1.1 million accounts. The Merrill Lynch service has five basic facets: a high yielding money market fund into which idle cash—dividends, interest or proceeds of securities sales—is automatically swept by computer; check writing privileges; access to brokerage services; a credit card or debit card for cash withdrawals; and a line of credit, usually in the form of a standard Wall Street margin account. Despite its success, the cash management account probably loses money for Merrill Lynch despite the enormous revenues it produces. Servicing it requires a great deal of capital—for people, computer systems, and a variety of processing and statement costs.

The securities industry has, as a result of these new products and services, substantially broadened its revenue sources so that brokerage commissions are now the third most important source of revenue. Commissions now account for 24.4 percent of revenue, down from 55.3 percent in 1973 (see Table 10.2).

The nature of the business is changing in other ways as well. Individuals deserted the stock market in droves as stock prices headed downward in the early 1970s but with the stock market

TABLE 10.2
Securities Industry Revenue Breakdown
(percent of total)

	1973	1977	1980	1981	1982 (9 mos.)
Brokerage commissions	55.3	41.8	35.4	27.0	24.4
Trading (including accrued interest on bond inventories and repurchase agreements)	8.4	19.3	23.0	24.3	27.0
Margin interest	13.4	11.2	13.0	15.0	10.3
Underwriting	9.0	11.6	8.2	8.0	9.0
All other (residual)	13.9	16.2	20.4	25.7	29.3

Some industry practitioners take exception to this analysis. They point out that brokerage commissions still rank as the largest non-interest source of revenue. Given the enormous volatility of markets, interest income could drop sharply if interest rates fall (as they have in the last half of 1982). As a result, brokerage commissions would increase significantly their relative importance.

Source: "Securities Industry Trends," Securities Industry Association, 8(6), November 2, 1982.

booming in the 1980s, they have begun to return. At the same time institutions increased their purchases of bonds and stocks as pension contributions swelled to over $20 billion per year in the early 1980s. Institutional trading now accounts for 76 percent of New York Stock Exchange trading volume, up from 59 percent in 1974, in contrast to individual trading which accounted for 24 percent in the third quarter of 1982 versus 41 percent in 1974 (see Table 10.3).

The development of new vehicles for venture capital investment is still another trend. This high risk area requires prudence on the part of the investor. Fortunes have been made but the risks of loss are very large. In 1981, a record $1.4 billion was invested in venture capital deals with an estimated $2.0 billion more invested in such deals in 1982.

TABLE 10.3
Breakdown of New York Stock Exchange Trading
(percent of daily volume estimated)

	1974	1976	1979	1980	1981	1982*
Institutional	59	58	65	67	70	76
Individual	41	42	35	33	30	24

*First half annualized.

Source: "Securities Industry Trends," a special paper by Joel Rosenthal, Vice President, Jesup & Lamont Securities Co., Inc. Securities Industry Association 8(7), November 2, 1982.

Financial Futures

Potentially the most important and significant new product area in the securities industry is financial futures and its older cousin, options trading. The irony is that options trading and financial futures were developed and prospered initially outside the securities industry. Both developments grew out of efforts by Chicago commodity traders to offset the decline in agricultural and extractive commodities trading which were historically the bulwark of the Chicago commodity markets. Financial futures and options trading have grown so rapidly that they now dwarf the commodity contracts traded on the commodity markets of the midwest. The need for financial futures contracts grew out of the increasing volatility of interest rates and the accompanying price fluctuation in fixed income instruments. As Gordon Donhowe, treasurer of Pillsbury Co., put it, "these days, the most volatile commodity we buy is cash, not wheat."[1]

In recent months, commercial banks and Wall Street securities firms have entered the financial futures markets as brokers and traders. Other financial institutions, such as pension funds and savings and loan associations, and some industrial corporations, have also entered the trading. As people in the futures business see it, the corporate potential for trading such vehicles is huge. "For every 500 industrial concerns, you may have 100 that need to hedge copper and 50 who may need to hedge grain but every one of them uses cash and therefore has a need to hedge the risk of fluctuation in interest rates," says Gary Perlin, a consultant in financial futures.[2]

The volume of trading in these futures is already huge, although industrial users are just beginning to use them to hedge their future cash needs. For example, Treasury bond futures trading presently totals $60 billion in contracts daily, two to three times the actual cash market in Treasury bonds.

As the Chicago Board of Trade sees it the major users of financial futures in the future will be:

Financial institutions—including commercial banks, thrift institutions, stock brokerages, pension funds and insurance companies. All these institutions have in common the need to hedge future values of financial instruments including certificates of deposits, Treasury and Federal Agency securities, inventories of common stock and debt securities, and to hedge "warehousing" positions in mortgages.

Nonfinancial firms seeking to hedge cash positions, commercial paper operations, raw material inventories, and foreign exchange operations.

One illustration of the use of financial futures was their use to hedge underwriter's positions in the disastrous IBM financing a few years ago. The market broke with the news that the Federal Reserve was going to tighten money and credit. Salomon Bros., one of the two managing underwriters, was able to avoid loss by selling futures contracts in advance of the deal to hedge its position.

Financial futures first began trading in the Chicago markets five years ago. By 1981 a total of 29 million contracts were traded, accounting for 29.4 percent of the total trading in futures contracts. Volume in 1982 represented an estimated 50 percent of total futures trading.

Only a few of new contracts generate significant volume so the exchanges are constantly experimenting with new contracts. The Chicago Mercantile Exchange, for example, is now designing a contract based on an index of corporate bonds.

PLACE STRATEGIES

As with most other financial service institutions, securities firms control their outlets of distribution. Branch office systems have spread over the entire world, firms such as Merrill Lynch and E. F. Hutton have hundreds of branches each. In 1982 all member firms of the New York Stock Exchange had 53,600 registered representatives working out of over 4,500 branch offices. The sprawling branch office system has the drawback of heavy fixed overhead expense in the long-term leases of these retail offices.

This high overhead is one of the reasons why many securities firms have sought mergers with capital-rich firms outside the securities business. Brokers typically commit for leases that can run 10 to 20 years in duration. These fixed commitments are still another reason why securities firms have concerned themselves with diversifying into relatively consistent sources of revenue to smooth the future fluctuations in profits (see Table 10.4).

The securities industry has been slowly moving towards a central reporting system that will consolidate all trading into a composite system of reporting securities transactions. The National Association of Securities Dealers (NASD) pioneered the development of a fully automated quotation system, known as NASDAQ. The NASDAQ system could handle the reporting and quotation of all stocks currently listed on the New York Stock Exchange and all other stock exchanges combined. One advantage to the investor is that NASDAQ features five to seven market makers in each over-the-counter stock listed versus only one market maker for stocks listed on the New York Stock Exchange. By having more than one market maker, stock traders in the over-the-counter market benefit from a more competitive market place. Trading in over-the-counter markets has reached a daily trading volume of 50 million shares.

As the firms broaden their offerings into new fields, the boundary lines between brokers, banks, and mutual funds are fast disappearing. Mergers are accelerating this trend, with many mergers involving firms from outside the securities business such as insurance companies and the retailing giants like Sears. If the Glass-Steagall Act is repealed, this would result in an increase in

TABLE 10.4
Volatility of Stock Trading and Profits

	Pre-tax Profits of NYSE Firms (in billions)	Average Daily NYSE Volume (in millions)
1966	$ 0.65	7.5
1967	1.09	10.1
1968	1.35	13.0
1969	0.59	11.4
1970	0.60	11.6
1971	1.15	15.4
1972	0.90	16.5
1973	0.06	16.1
1975	0.82	18.6
1976	0.95	21.2
1977	0.42	20.9
1978	0.68	28.6
1979	1.10	32.2
1980	2.27	44.9
1981	2.14	46.8
1982 (Est.)	3.00	65.4

Source: "Facts Book", New York Stock Exchange, 1982 and earlier editions.

bank acquisitions of securities firms. Inevitably, these mergers accentuate the conflicts of interest inherent in the financial service field and raise the specter of renewed regulation if the conflicts result in abuses.

Another trend spurred on by the increase in institutional investing has been the growth of specialty Wall Street broker firms providing specific information on emerging growth areas of the economy and market and technical information to help institutional investors. Most of these services are paid for by brokerage commissions, directed to the brokers supplying the information by the institutions receiving and benefiting from this information.

PRICE STRATEGIES

The freeing up of stock exchange commissions had a major impact on the securities business. The Securities and Exchange Commission, when they pushed for removal of fixed rates, thought the ensuing competition would reduce brokerage fees for individuals as well as institutions. The SEC now admits the opposite result occurred. Rates for individuals have increased since the unfixing of rates, while rates for institutional investors have declined dramatically. The lower rates for institutions have made mutual funds more attractive as an investing intermediary for individuals because they gain the advantage of volume purchasing of stocks. Commissions and fees vary widely, especially between institutional and individual customers. Institutions, with their huge buying power, control the pricing mechanism. In fact, the institutions refrained from pushing stock broker commissions too low, so that the securities firms could make a profit and remain as important suppliers of services to the institutions which depend on Wall Street.

During the chaotic period of price cutting following "May Day" the SEC wondered whether the big firms were engaging in predatory pricing, the practice of selling at a loss with the intent of driving out the competition. The extreme price cutting has now abated and the industry is making record profits from the huge trading volumes which have seen the 100 million share day become commonplace in the 1980s.

Brokers have been unbundling their commission charges so that they charge separately for research services, transactions, security custody, stock margin credit, and in some cases for inactivity in a brokerage account. Several brokers, including E. F. Hutton, have pioneered a flat annual fee which bundles up all securities transactions including investment management. Hutton's fee is 3 percent per annum. This arrangement eliminates the incentive to churn an account. At the same time it weakens the allegiance between the individual broker and the client. Many stock brokers are uneasy about this arrangement, fearing it is a step by the firms to drive a wedge between themselves and their clients. However, this idea of eliminating commissions, and thereby eliminating client fears about churning, is a very marketable idea whose time may be coming.

PROMOTION STRATEGIES

Over 30 years ago, in 1949, Louis Engel, a young marketing executive with Merrill Lynch set the tone of advertising for his firm and for the securities industry for years to come. Mr. Engel believed that brokers should revise their marketing strategies and drastically step up their advertising efforts because they could no longer depend on doing business with just a handful of the rich and financially literate. Merrill Lynch has followed this basic philosophy since that time and is the major success story of the securities business, much emulated by its envious competitors.

The advertising of most securities firms emphasizes the service provided by the broker and any specific services or reports that are available from that broker. Limited use has been made of advertising claiming exceptional performance results, this restraint presumably resulting from the strict New York Stock Exchange restrictions designed to curb performance claims based on past records.

Broker advertising has tended to project an image. Merrill Lynch's bull image is meant to convey the firm's basic optimism in the future growth of America and the prospect for profitable investment in U.S. industry. Shearson/American Express describes itself as "the new flagship of the financial world" in its new advertising campaign launched in 1982. According to Shearson's agency, Grey Advertising, Shearson will be spending $6 million on the new campaign, twice the amount spent last year. In spending, however, Merrill Lynch dwarfs its competitors, promoting its "bullish" image with $13 million for broadcast advertising and another $10 million for print media.

The primary promotion system, however, remains individual salespersons. Registered representatives are the heart of the distribution system. Commission payments to registered representatives rose to about 40 percent of the gross commission produced in recent years versus 30 percent which was typical for many decades. Much pirating of brokers has taken place during the past ten years because of the rising costs of training new salesmen and the need to bring in proven producers to help pay for the aforementioned overhead expenses. New York Stock Exchange rules require that member firms train a new broker for at least six months and that each new salesperson take a rigorous qualifying examination to become a registered representative. It is estimated that it costs a member firm about $20,000 to train and qualify a new registered representative.

Member firms have been trying to reduce their dependence on the individual salesman by developing a more direct allegiance with the client. Traditionally the customer thinks of his representative as the "firm." Thus, when a salesman changed firms, he was able to transfer most of his accounts from his old firm to his new one. Firms, through advertising, are trying to develop an image with the customers directly, thus weakening the traditional allegiance to the registered representative. This strategy has taken on additional urgency as the level of "piracy" between firms escalates.

NOTES

1. "Financial Futures Surge as Banks, Industrial Firms Move Into Market," *Wall Street Journal*, March 23, 1982.

2. *Ibid.*

ELEVEN

Investment Banking

THE STRUCTURE OF THE INDUSTRY

One entrepreneur in the field describes the creative aspect of investment banking as analogous to "a tailor who starts with a button and makes a suit," instead of starting with a pattern and cloth and then making the suit. In other words, the investment banker adds the element of creativity critical to every specialized financing situation. Investment bankers "make their suits" in a variety of ways, ranging from underwriting to private venture deals. The breakdown in recent years can be seen in Table 11.1.

Commercial banks have increased their activities in investment banking despite the apparent ban on such activities under the Glass-Steagall Act. The Act permits the banks to underwrite municipal general obligation bonds, engage in the private placement of corporate securities with institutional investors, arrange mergers and acquisitions for corporate clients, and engage in financial advisory activities for their corporate finance clients. Commercial banks would like to enlarge their investment banking role and are lobbying actively for a change in the Glass-Steagall Act to permit them to underwrite revenue bonds issued by state and local governments.

Be that as it may, commercial banks face a tough battle with

TABLE 11.1
Investment Banking Deals in Recent Years
(in billions of dollars)

Type	1975	1976	1977	1978	1979	1980	1981	1982*
Underwriting	47	42	37	31	37	58	63	76
Private placements	14	21	26	24	23	16	18	22
Mergers & Acquisitions	12	20	22	34	44	44	83	54
Muncipal underwritings	30	35	47	48	43	48	55	70
Venture capital deals	NA**	NA	NA	0.4	0.4	0.9	1.4	2.0

*Estimated by author.

**NA-not applicable.

Source: Various financing directories published by *the Investment Dealer's Digest,* Copyright IDD, Inc. 1982.

investment bankers in their attempts to expand their financing activities. Interviews with a cross-section of corporate financial executives indicate that most banks have not made much headway with industry in the permissible areas of investment banking because of negative perceptions. Bankers are thought to be unimaginative, perceived to be people who could not make it in Wall Street. Other reservations about commercial bankers include the fear that bankers can not be trusted with confidential information and that they tend to steer clear of hostile takeover fights for fear of alienating potential loan customers on the other side; to concern that they lack recognition from their commercial banker bosses.[1]

Mergers and acquisitions are growing rapidly as a financing vehicle in the investment banking field. Business corporations find that they can expand their operations or achieve desirable diversification more economically by acquiring another company, given the extreme low market valuation for corporate common stock over the past ten years, a condition that was substantially corrected in the latter half of 1982. Merger deals exceeded public offerings in 1981 for the first time in recent memory but then fell behind new public offerings in the booming stock and bond market of 1982.

In the field of underwritten public offerings, the large investment banking houses are significantly increasing their market share at the expense of the smaller regional firms (see Table 11.2).

The entrée of retail stock brokers into investment banking is another trend. This has caused an upheaval in the traditional wholesale dominance of investment banking distribution. Historically, wholesale houses such as Morgan Stanley, Lehman, Kuhn Loeb, and Goldman Sachs arranged the underwritings and then formed syndicates of regional and national stock brokerage firms to distribute the securities purchased by the syndicate to the investing public. Now with the entrée of giant national retail firms such as Merrill Lynch, E.F. Hutton, and Paine Webber, the wholesale investment banker's predominant role in distribution has been weakened somewhat.

Now, a giant firm such as Shearson/American Express backed by the financial resources of American Express can underwrite an entire issue and distribute it through its many retail outlets located

TABLE 11.2
Concentration in Underwriting
(market share in percent of total volume of offerings)

Year	Top 10 Firms	Top 25 Firms
1976	46.2	66.4
1977	47.8	79.2
1978	50.7	75.3
1979	49.1	70.9
1980	53.1	75.3
1981	50.3	73.0
1982 (9 mos.)	58.2	80.4

Source: "Securities Industry Trends," Securities Industry Association, 8(6), November 2, 1982.

in every nook and cranny of the country. The evidence of this erosion of the wholesale banker's position is more apparent than real, however, as a glance at the composition of the top ten underwriting firms in 1982 in Table 11.3 reveals. As indicated, wholesale houses comprised five of the ten largest underwriting firms in 1982. Nevertheless, the distribution function is gaining relative to origination. This trend should continue to grow as Rule 415 deals gain ascendancy.

Equity financing deals continue to be relatively small in relation to bond deals. This is true in most periods except during rampant speculative markets, such as those in the 1980s, when equity deals picked up relative to bond deals (see Table 11.4).

Except during periods of intense speculation bond deals usually account for over 70 percent of the financing arranged by investment banking syndicates and close to 100 percent of their private placements (see Table 11.5).

The fundamental advantage bond financing has over stock deals is that bond interest is tax-deductible and common stock dividends are not; therefore the net cost of financing through debt is lower with bond financing.

Moreover, common stock values have been so low over the past decade that the dividend cost of equity financing has risen relative to the after tax cost of bond financing. Finally, during

TABLE 11.3
Top Ten Managing Underwriting Firms in 1982
(in billions of dollars)

Morgan Stanley*	14.3
Salomon Bros.*	12.5
Merrill Lynch	10.8
Goldman Sachs*'	10.0
First Boston Corp.*	7.2
Lehman, Kuhn Loeb*	5.0
Blyth Eastman Paine Webber	3.4
Drexel Burnham Lambert	2.3
Kidder, Peabody	2.1
Dean Witter Reynolds	2.0

*Wholesale underwriting house all underwriting.
Source: Investment Dealers' Digest, March 11, 1983, p. 6, copyright IDD, Inc., 1983.

TABLE 11.4
Underwritten Public Offerings
(in billions of dollars)

Year	Bonds	Preferred	Equity	Totals
1973	13.4	2.4	6.9	22.7
1974	27.3	1.7	2.6	31.6
1975	37.0	3.0	6.8	46.8
1976	32.0	2.2	8.1	42.4
1977	27.6	2.5	6.6	36.7
1978	23.4	1.7	6.0	31.2
1979	28.9	2.0	5.7	36.6
1980	41.6	3.2	13.3	58.2
1981	47.0	1.7	15.0	63.7
1982	54.9	5.2	15.9	76.0

Source: "Corporate Financing Directory," 1982 edition, as updated in January 11, 1983 issue, p. 3, Investment Dealers' Digest, copyright IDD, Inc. 1983.

TABLE 11.5
Private Placements of Corporate Securities
(in billions of dollars)

Year	Bonds	Preferred	Equity	Totals
1973	10.6	1.3	0.4	12.2
1974	9.7	0.5	0.5	10.7
1975	12.9	0.3	0.3	13.5
1976	20.5	0.5	0.2	21.2
1977	23.7	1.9	0.2	25.8
1978	21.8	1.6	0.1	23.5
1979	19.7	2.7	0.1	22.5
1980	14.5	1.5	0.3	16.3
1981	16.7	1.0	0.6	18.2
1982	18.8	0.9	0.4	22.3*

*Includes $2.2 billion in other equity financing included in limited partnership deals.

Source: "Corporate Financing Directory, 1982 edition, as updated in January 11, 1983 edition, Investment Dealers' Digest, copyright IDD, Inc. 1983.

inflationary periods, bond financing permits the corporation to pay back the bond holders in depreciated dollars. Common stock financing could return to favor in the future, should these factors change.

Bond offerings are proliferating in style as well as in volume. Many innovative arrangements have been created by investment bankers to make bond deals even more attractive to investors, among them equity kickers (warrants and options to purchase stock), floating rate bonds (to prevent fluctuations in bond prices), shorter maturities (to reduce the inflationary risk to investors), and zero coupon bonds (that appeal to tax-deferred retirement plans because the future return is "locked in"). "Zeros" also permit the corporation to finance without paying interest until the bonds mature, at which point the inflationary impact may greatly reduce the burden of repayment. Another fairly complicated procedure involves swapping stock for existing highly discounted low coupon bonds enabling the corporation to reduce its debt at costs considerably under the maturity value of the bonds and substitute low dividend paying stock that improves the debt-equity ratio.

Investment banking is probably the last sector of the financial service industry where fixed rates will continue into the fore-seeable future. There have been several challenges to the fixed rate structure in the past, usually on anti-trust grounds. However, the economic justification for fixed rates of offering during the public distribution of securities underwritten by an investment banking syndicate override any theory that the public would benefit from competitive rates during these syndicated offerings. When an investment banking syndicate agrees to underwrite the securities of a corporation, it provides needed funds for corporate growth and expansion. The corporation is assured of the availability of the funds on a known basis and agrees to the syndication with the investment bankers. Once the deal is set, the underwriters own the securities being marketed—as opposed to a broker who does not take title to the securities he sells—and the investment bankers, therefore, take on the market risk of price declines in the underwritten security.

IBM'S OCTOBER 1979 DEBT OFFERING

The IBM debt offering of October 1979 is a dramatic illustration of the nature and risks of modern investment banking and underwriting. IBM's debt offering, the largest in U.S. history up to that time, consisted of $500 million in seven-year notes and $500 million in 25 year debentures for a total of $1 billion.

Salomon Bros. and Merrill Lynch headed the underwriting syndicate that brought the bonds to market in the fall of 1979. During the period of negotiation with the underwriters the prime rate increased five times, reaching 13.5 percent at the end of September. With rapidly rising yields, the deal was finally brought to market on Thursday, October 4th. The notes were priced at 9.62 percent and the debentures at 9.41 percent with an underwriting spread of five-eighths of 1 percent on the notes and seven-eighths of 1 percent on the debentures. On Saturday, October 6th, the Federal Reserve announced an increase in the discount rate and a number of credit-tightening policies described as "draconian" in the financial press. On the Monday following, the bond market fell sharply and the underwriters disbanded the syndicate to permit each syndicate member to fend for themselves. The IBM notes and debentures dropped about five points each resulting in losses which were estimated as high as $20 million to the underwriters who still held an estimated $300 to $400 million of unsold bonds at the time the syndicate was abandoned. But IBM was paid for the bonds on time and in the amount agreed. The IBM offering illustrates that underwriting risks are real and investment bankers provide corporations with a worthwhile means of arranging large financings.

In the most recent attack on the fixed rate system, referred to in Wall Street as the "Papilsky case", the courts ruled in favor of the underwriters but the National Association of Securities Dealers and the Securities and Exchange Commission have modified the rules somewhat to provide for more effective pricing monitoring to assure that underwriting rates are realistic.

More recently the SEC has taken the lead in weakening the fixed rate system through the forced competition embodied in the new experimental registration procedures under SEC Rules 415. This rule promotes developing a system of so-called "shelf registrations" which permits corporations to shop their corporate financings for up to 24 months with complete flexibility as to prices, terms and offering date. Shelf registration financings had been growing under a previous rule (SEC Rule S 16). This rule, introduced in 1979, also permits liberalized registration procedures for large companies. S 16 offerings accounted for about 70% of all underwritten offerings in 1981.

Rule 415 permits the 1,300 largest companies in the country (meeting the minimum market capitalization of $100 million) to file proposed offerings which remain in effect for up to 24 months from the filing date. Reference to annual reports and 10K filings update the registration automatically. The company can then offer the block piecemeal whenever it feels it has a good offer. The effect of Rule 415 has been to drive down investment banking fees and to spur new financing. A negative aspect is that it has weakened the investment banker's "due diligence" function and has shifted the balance of power in corporate financing from Wall Street to the corporate executive suite. The disastrous market performance of an equity offering of Continental Illinois Bank last summer, following the tardy disclosure by the bank of bad debt exposure and resulting poor earnings, illustrate the continuing need for vigorous due diligence by investment bankers to protect the public. Naturally, with so much at stake, investment bankers are very concerned with the future implications of Rule 415 on their businesses and have tried to have the rule modified or aborted if possible. Rule 415 deals accounted for $16 billion, equal to one-third of total bond deals, in 1982, the first year of its use. It would appear that the rule will be permanently adopted. Rule 415 will probably transform investment banking from syndication to "bought" deals with the investment banker acting more as a principal dealer than a syndicator. "Bought" deals are growing in popularity in Western Europe. Despite all the protests from the major investment bankers, they appeared to be the leading participant in Rule 415 financings in 1982. One wonders whether there is some truth in the saying, "the more things change, the more they stay the same."

PRODUCT STRATEGIES

Investment banker serve their clients in myriad ways. These include:

Fee Studies—Through fee studies, they advise new clients on how they should finance their growth in the future. These studies provide a blueprint for a corporate financial officer and usually lead to a long run investment banking relationship.

Underwritings—These are the most visible part of any investment banking relationship. They constitute the taking of risk to provide long-term financing to a corporation through the purchase of the corporation's securities by the investment banker and their subsequent resale to the public through an investment banking syndication.

Private Venture Capital Deals—these usually provide capital to fledging enterprises that an investment banker finds attractive but that are still unseasoned for public distribution. Usually the lead banker will show the deal to a number of friendly investment bankers with similar interests to see if they feel the fledgling company has enough long-term attractiveness to warrant an investment of private capital. If these knowledgeable and reliable sources find the company to their liking, than the lead banker will go ahead and invest jointly the monies in the venture, looking towards the day when the firm will be ready for public sale and the private capital can be liquidated at a profit. With the new shelf registration rules increasing competition and reducing the traditional role of investment bankers, many underwriting firms have moved to start venture capital partnerships or closed-end trusts so that they can develop investment banking relationships from the start up stage (see Table 11.6).

Venture capital pools are comprised of four distinct types of investors:

1) Private capital funds, the oldest type, continue the financing interest of the very wealthy families and the small, highly specialized investment banking firms. Venrock (the family fund for the Rockefeller clan), Hambrecht & Quist and Allen & Co. are examples of this type of fund. These groups like to get involved at an early stage and help out in the development of an idea from "seed" to public offering, a process that can take up to ten years to come to fruition.

TABLE 11.6
Wall Street's Entrée into Venture Capital

Investment banker	Venture Capital Fund	Assets (in millions of dollars)
Morgan Stanley	Kleiner Perkins Caufield & Byers III of San Francisco (Affiliate)	150
Dillon, Read	Concord Partners	80
Merrill Lynch	M.L. Ventures Partners I	60
Goldman Sachs	Morgan, Holland, Fund of Boston (Affiliate)	58.5
Alex Brown & Sons	ABF Ventures L. P.	26
L.F. Rothschild, Unterberg, Towbin	L.F. Rothschild, Unterberg, Towbin Ventures	14

Source: "Venture Capital Lures Old-line Investment Banks," *The New York Times*, November 7, 1982, © 1981/82 by The New York Times Company. Reprinted by permission.

2) Business corporations like Dupont, Textron, General Motors, Eastman Kodak, and Xerox finance start-up ideas partly for profit but mainly to keep an interest in emerging technologies on an "arm's length" basis.
3) Commercial banks either directly or through their wholly-owned small business investment companies (SBIC) have become the largest of the venture capital sources. Citibank and Bank of America are two of the most active participants.
4) Finally, a disparate group representing many diverse interests, including pension funds, consulting firms, New York Stock Exchange brokers, and large investment banking firms.

As aforementioned, originating investment bankers have moved to acquire, or affiliate with, specialized venture capital firms. This move by the wholesalers seems to be aimed at gaining greater control over the emerging small companies as primary prospects for the future financing role of the originating houses. Faced with the loss of their Fortune 500 corporate finance accounts as a result of increasingly competitive pricing growing out of SEC Rules S 16 and 415 registrations, wholesale houses appear to be shifting their focus to the smaller companies as investment banking clients in the future.

Mergers and Acquisitions—These activities represent the most rapidly growing sector of the investment banking business. Equity markets have been depressed until recently, frequently below the book value of a corporation. Thus, a company seeking to expand or diversify in a certain field would be well advised to look into the possibility of a merger or acquisition as an attractive method of expanding. The acquired company usually is offered more than market value in the merger offer making the deal attractive to the selling stockholders. Deals can be financed by exchange of stock avoiding the capital gains tax in most cases. Mergers and acquisitions have provided much revenue for investment bankers in recent years. Moreover, commercial banks, which are forbidden by law from public underwritings of corporate securities, can arrange mergers and acquisitions as an alternative. This is a competitive area and investment bankers are predominant because of their creative expertise and because they do not have the built-in conflicts which beset a commercial bank. Banks, for example, usually do not want to participate in hostile take-overs involving tender offers because they frequently find that the target of the takeover attempt may be a good corporate loan account of the bank.

Private Placements—This financing technique traditionally finds its major use with small and medium-sized corporations that are not seasoned enough for the public underwriting market but need capital for expansion and growth. While interest rates tend to be higher in the private placement market (over 90 percent of private placements are debt offerings), the costs are lower. The expenses of a public offering are avoided because private deals bypass the need for prospectuses and other heavy legal,filing and wire expenses involved in a public deal. Insurance companies and pension funds are the primary investors in the private placement field. They find the interest rate differentials attractive and frequently warrants or other equity kickers are included in the deals. In recent years, however, insurance companies have cut back on private placements because of negative cash flows resulting from the sharp increase in policyholder loans stimulated by the very low rates on such loans.

PRICE STRATEGIES

Fixed price dominates in the investment banking field. Fees for underwriting vary with the degree of risk, from 8 to 10 percent for equity deals to as little as 1 percent or less for utility and bond offerings. Finders fees on deals, that is the fees made by individuals who bring deals to the attention of investment bankers, are usually one-half of 1 percent of the investment bankers fee or less, depending on the size of the deal. Fees for private studies can run $50,000 to $500,000. Fees for the efforts of investment bankers in a merger or acquisition transaction run much higher, as much as 5 percent of the value of the transaction depending on the size of the deal and the amount of difficulty involved in the negotiation.

One can assume that fixed pricing will yield to competitive pressures brought on by SEC Rule 415, the experimental registration rule that permits large corporations to file blocks of securities for sale for periods up to 24 months.

PLACE STRATEGIES

Most deals are brought to investment bankers by finders, regional brokers and corporate finance specialists within the investment banking firm. Outside sources are extremely valuable. They know the local needs for financing better than the investment bank staff, which is of necessity tied up at the home office on other financings. Small country banks that can not handle the financing needs of a client will frequently pass deals along to investment bankers in return for some form of remuneration.

Distribution of investment banking syndicates can be arranged through selling syndicates which comprise hundreds of small regional houses bound together with the lead underwriter in a syndiation, or they can be done in-house through a national broker network of registered representatives of one firm, such as Merrill Lynch, without other firms in the syndication. Frequently, the investment banker will arrange to place part of the financing directly with large institutional or private investors, bypassing altogether the need to underwrite the securities. These types of deals are likely to increase in the future as investment bankers get used to life under Rule 415. In this type of transaction the investment banker acts as an agent for the corporation, receiving a fee for the securities placed. In a Rule 415 purchase the investment banker would be acting as a principal, hoping to place the securities with an institutional buyer at a profit. The investment banker could of course bid under Rule 415 offerings for all or part of a block of securities offered by a corporation with the intention of forming a syndicate to take down the securities and distribute them as in traditional offerings. However, with "bought" deals or "Dutch" auctions, it is not likely that the spread will permit the use of the syndicate route. Speed will be necessary to reduce the investment banker's risk.

PROMOTION STRATEGIES

Top executives of investment banks continuously canvass the regional firms, banks, and local contacts to find new and interesting deals. Wholesale houses depend on the regional dealer network to make up the backbone of the distribution system, once an investment banking syndicate is formed. One of the major trends in the business is the decline of wholesale houses. This is partly a result of the decline in the number of regional firms as they fall prey to the expansion of national retail networks, and partly to the reality that the power in corporate finance has shifted from Wall Street to the corporate suite on Park Avenue. Regional firms are being absorbed, at prices attractive to the selling partners, for much the same reason the big corporations are acquiring going businesses rather than starting new operations. The national firms are thriving, with far flung retail networks that enhance their ability to dispose of large blocks of securities quickly and efficiently.

Advertising is used little in this field because the amounts involved are large and the personal sales approach is vital to success, in terms of finding deals as well as selling them. Some institutional advertising is used in prestige business and financial publications such as *Fortune*, and *Institutional Investor*, but the most frequently appearing investment bank advertising is the ubiquitous tombstone advertisement that investment bankers proudly publish to announce a completed investment banking transaction. Very little product advertising is used as the field is too complex and varied.

NOTE

1. "The Banks' Uphill Battle against Investment Bankers" Neil Osborn, *Institutional Investor*, May 1981.

TWELVE

Conclusions

The pace of change is so rapid in the financial service field that predictions for the future are nearly impossible to make. With this caveat, the author will look into his crystal ball to see what lies ahead.

FINANCIAL MARKETS

The rampant volatility of financial markets will dictate much of the future. Most economic forecasters believe that inflation, coupled with stagnant growth and productivity, will continue to be the nation's primary economic problem over the decade of the 1980s.

Given these assumptions, interest rates should continue historically high and the wide swings in prices in the capital markets will cause investors to seek hedges against market declines. A new world of financial options has grown in response to this need. These financial options will grow in volume rivaling the conventional trading in securities. In fact, at present, stock option contracts exceed the value of the trading in the underlying securities they represent on the New York Stock Exchange.

COMPETITION

Competition will tend to force smaller financial service units to seek out merger partners and this will bring in its wake a diversified offering of financial services. The investor, rooted in the traditional specialty store approach in buying financial services, will probably take a long time to change his preferences to the department store approach, if ever. But the efficiencies of the computer dictate that mass merchandising of these specialized services is the wave of the future.

CONFLICTS OF INTEREST

The author believes the risk of abuse of the special conflicts of interest inherent in financial transactions requires continuing major safeguards. Obviously, the financial department store of the future will have to address these concerns and find answers that protect the public interest and at the same time achieve the distribution economies feasible through mass merchandising. Mass merchandisers like Sears will find promising opportunities in these trends.

REGULATION

The trend toward deregulation of the financial service industry will continue apace, whether a Democrat or a Republican occupies the White House. The cleansing effects of publicity and industry self-regulation probably will largely replace the need for federal regulation. The SEC probably will become more a criminal fraud "watchdog" agency rather than a pure regulatory agency.

The Glass-Steagall Act and the McFadden Act will gradually be amended, giving banks the opportunity to diversify both in terms of services offered as well as regional access. Unit banking will go the way of the horse and buggy.

MARKET RESEARCH

Meaningful research will replace the "seat of the pants" approach to new product development. While it is true that new product launches in this industry are far less expensive than in the package goods industry, with the size of the financial service units becoming larger and competition increasing, the need for more efficiency in new product development should cause market research to become the rule for most of the large firms in the field. This should be enhanced by the trend toward concentration apparent in the industry today. Prestige is an important consideration for financial service firms. A failed product for a small firm is acceptable but damaging to the prestige of a large firm. Sears and the other nonfinancial firms will bring a considerable degree of market research expertise to the financial service field.

FADING BOUNDARY LINES

The continuing mergers of financial service firms has changed the character of Wall Street. Boundary lines are blurring. Small firms are being absorbed by larger units. The original star system which identified and segmented the investment business is rapidly giving way to the managerial system with its committees and bureaucracy. Creativity is probably being smothered to some extent by the emergence of financial giants. Despite all this, small specialty firms will continue to spring up to provide special services and to prosper among the behemoths. This trend is consistent with other industries that have grown in size while spawning smaller specialty firms in their wake.

CONSUMER PREFERENCES AND PERCEPTIONS

While insurance companies may offer the same services as banks, mutual funds, and stock brokers they will continue to look like insurance companies to the consumer because each financial service unit will try to maintain a distinctive image. The public perceives Prudential as a giant life insurance company and Merrill Lynch as a stock broker even though they have become financial congenerics. No amount of advertising can change these images in the public's mind. Thus it is important for purveyors of financial services to capitalize on the public's perceptions of their businesses. The image problem will probably most severely affect the nonfinancial companies—the retailers and industrial companies— that wish to enter the financial service industry. Their image will be inconsistent with the value of the financial services they seek to offer.

CAREER OPPORTUNITIES

Career opportunities will continue to escalate in the financial service field. Particular emphasis will be on individuals with advanced degrees in business administration, law, computer technology, and accounting—the backbones of the financial service field. It is probable that some of the business schools in the financial centers of New York, Boston, and Chicago will develop a special MBA program for the financial service industry.

Bibliography

BOOKS

Berry, Leonard L. *Financial Institutions Marketing Strategies in the 1980s.* Washington, D.C.: Consumer Bankers Association, 1980.

Goldberg, Lawrence G., and Lawrence J. White. *The Deregulation of the Banking and Securities Industries*, Lexington, Mass.: Lexington Books (D. C. Heath), 1979.

McCarthy, E. Jerome, *Basic Marketing: A Managerial Approach*, (Sixth Edition) Homewood, Ill., Richard D. Irwin, 1978.

BANKING PUBLICATIONS

Asher, Joe. "Five Cards for One Bank? Yes, Says City National Bank, Columbus, Ohio." *Banking*, May 1977, pp. 39–41, 130.

Benzer, Robert F.. "The EFT Act: Marketing Implication and Consideration." *Bank Marketing*, March 1979, pp. 20–25, 44.

——. "Retail Banking in the 80s—A Smaller Slice of a Bigger Pie." *Bank Marketing*, December 1979, pp. 21–24.

Carcione, Sandra G. "Are You Ready for Nationwide NOWs?" *Bank Marketing*, January 1980, pp. 16–19.

Dupuy, George M. "Segmenting the Trust Market by Design, Not Default." *Trusts and Estates*, July 1980, pp. 35–38.

Greene, Joel N. "How to Use Trust Marketing Research." *Trusts and Estates*, June 1980, pp. 29–36.

Ingram, Jerry F., and Olin S. Pugh. "Consumer Usage of Financial Services." *The Bankers Magazine*, July/August 1981, pp. 40–53.

Loy, David, and Ike Mathur. "The Pricing and Quality of Commercial Banking Services." *The Bankers Magazine*, July/August 1981, pp. 33–37.

Mears, Peter, Frederick Siegel, and Robert Osborn. "How to Find Out What Customers Want from Their Bank." *The Bankers Magazine*, July/August 1981, pp. 67–71.

Reynolds, John J. "The Plastic Card: How Big a Role in Retail Banking?" *Bank Marketing*, April 1979, pp. 20–24.

Roderique, Ronald J., "Product Development: Not for Big Banks Only." *Bank Marketing*, May 1980, pp. 12–15.

Sullivan, Michael P. "Bank Marketing Strategy—Past, Present, and Future." *The Bankers Magazine*, July/August 1981, pp. 28–32.

Goodman, E. C., Jr. and Robert E. Wilkes. "A Technique to Aid Market Positioning." *Bank Marketing*, June 1980, pp. 14–17.

"The Personal Banker." *The Banker Magazine*, January-February 1978, pp. 54–55.

"Special Report/Marketing." *Banking*, May 1976, entire issue.

BUSINESS AND FINANCIAL PUBLICATIONS

"A Hard-Sell Strategy at Hutton." *Business Week*, January 19, 1981, pp. 109–110.

Brenner, Lynn. "Must Broker and Underwriter Merge to Survive?" *Institutional Investor*, June 1981, pp. 165–176.

"Battle of the Brokers." *Barron's*, November 1, 1982.

"Can American Express and Shearson Live Happily after the Merger." *Business Week*, May 18, 1981, pp. 106–114.

Cantor, Richard A. "Why Banks Have Trouble Managing Investment Accounts," *Institutional Investor*, September 1968.

Chakravarty, Subrata N. "Blast Furnace Banker." *Forbes*, October 26, 1981, pp. 95–98.

"Clash of the Credit Cards." *Dun's Review*, June 1978, pp. 94–100.

"Deals of the Year." *Fortune*, January 25, 1982, pp. 36–40.

"Electronic Banking—Network for Retail Banking Making Money from Transactions." *Business Week*, January 28, 1982, pp. 70–80.

Feinberg, Phyllis. "The Restructuring Game." *Institutional Investor*, February 1981, pp. 85–92.

_____. "The Battle over Revenue Bonds." *Institutional Investor*, October 1980, pp. 188–99..

Hill, Susan. "The Assault on the Independent Agent." *Institutional Investor*, July 1981, pp. 93–108.

_____. "Should Portfolio Managers Do Marketing?" *Institutional Investor*, June 1981, pp. 65–74.

"Housing's Storm: The Squeeze on Builders, Lenders, and Buyers." *Business Week*, September 7, 1981, pp. 60–66.

Jansson, Solveig. "The Feeling Is Mutual." *Institutional Investor*, November 1980, pp. 143–54.

"Look, Ma, No Commissions!" *Financial World*, February 15, 1980, pp. 54–56.

Loomis, Carole J., "The Shakeout on Wall Street Isn't Over Yet." *Fortune*, May 22, 1978, pp. 58–66.

_____. "Where Does Wall Street's Shakeout Leave Its Customers?" *Fortune*, June 19, 1978, pp. 140–48.

_____. "The Fight for Financial Turf." *Fortune*, December 28, 1981, pp. 54–65.

Morrison, Ann M. "The Venture Capitalist Who Tries to Win Them All." *Fortune*, February 2, 1980, pp. 96–99.

"Mutual Funds Resurge." *Business Week*, March 31, 1980, pp. 68–78.

O'Donnell, Thomas. "The Tube, the Card, the Ticker and Jim Robinson." *Forbes*, May 25, 1981, pp. 100–06.

Osborn, Neil. "The Banks' Uphill Battle against Investment Bankers." *Institutional Investor*, May 1981, pp. 50–60.

_____. "What Happens after Glass-Steagall?" *Institutional Investor*, February 1982, pp. 67–78.

Phalon, Richard. "Ned Johnson of FMR: Watch Your Flank, Merrill Lynch." *Forbes*, October 26, 1981, pp. 158–62.

Regan, Donald, "What's Wrong with Glass-Steagall." *Institutional Investor*, October 1981, pp. 21–22.

Rose, Sanford. "Checkless Banking Is Bound to Come." *Fortune*, June 1977, pp. 118–30.

_____. "More Bang for the Buck: The Magic of Electronic Banking." *Fortune*, May 1977, pp. 202–26.

Smith, Lee. "The High Rollers of First Boston." *Fortune*, September 6, 1982, pp. 55–60.

Thackray, John. "Is the Venture Capital Boom Getting Out of Hand?" *Institutional Investor*, November 1981, pp. 201–16.

"The Changing Life Insurers: New High Yield Products Mean High-risk Investments." *Business Week*, September 14, 1981, pp. 66–71.

"The Marketing Effort: Here's a Look at How to Sell Investment Services to Pension Funds. And, How Not to." *Institutional Investor*, July 1981, pp. 145–48.

"The New Banking Forces New Strategies." *Business Week*, July 13, 1981, pp. 56–61.

"The New Sears: Unable to Grow in Retailing, It Turns to Financial Services." *Business Week*, November 16, 1981, pp. 140–46.

"The New World of Corporate Finance." *Dun's Review*, August 1982.

"Upheavals in Investment Banking." *Fortune*, August 23, 1982

"Wholesale Banking's New Hard Sell." *Business Week*, April 13, 1981, pp. 82–86.

INSURANCE PUBLICATIONS

Autin, A. Anthony, Jr. "Product Change: The Challenge of the 1980s." *Best's Review*, July 1980, pp. 22–24, 78.

Cuscaden, Michael F. "Developing New Life Products." *Best's Review*, July 1979, pp. 71–74.

Dutter, Philip H. "The Coming Life Insurance Shakeup: Who Will Survive?" *CLU Journal*, October 1981, pp. 10–16.

Forbes, Steven W. "Forecast for the Life Insurance Industry." *Best's Review*, September 1981, pp. 10, 147–50.

Goldberg, Irwin W. "Insurance Industry Marketing Trends." *Best's Review*, July 1980, pp. 10–12, 73–78.

Greene, Mark R. "Marketing Property/Casualty Insurance: A Look Back and a Look Ahead." *Best's Review*, October 1980, pp. 14–18, 75–76, 81–84.

Ham, Michael J. "The Profit Impact of Market Strategy on the Insurance Industry." *Best's Review*, August 1980, pp. 22–24, 89–90.

Jaffe, Jay M. "The Impact of Bank Credit Cards on Insurance Marketing." *Best's Review*, October 1980, pp. 24, 29, 107–10.

"Life Insurance Update: Time to Take Another Look at Your Programs." *Association Management*, January 1981, pp. 65–67.

Sullivan, Frank E. "What's Ahead for the Life Insurance Industry for the Rest of the 1980s." *Weekly Underwriter*, January 10, 1981, pp. 20, 55–56.

PROFESSIONAL JOURNALS

Anderson, W. Thomas, Jr., Eli P. Cox III, and David G. Fulcher. "Bank Selection Decisions and Market Segmentation." *Journal of Marketing*, 40, January 1976, pp. 40–45.

Fraser, Donald R., "The Money Market, A Financial Intermediary." *MSU Business Topics*, 25(2), pp. 5–11, Graduate School of Business Administration, Michigan State University.

Hayes, Samuel L., III, "The Transformation of Investment Banking." *Harvard Business Review*, January-February 1979, pp. 153–70.

Johnson, Robert W. "Pricing of Bank Card Services." *Journal of Retail Banking*, June 1979, pp. 16–22.

Kielrulff, Herbert E. "Finding the Best Acquisition Candidate." *Harvard Business Review*, January-February 1981, pp. 66–68.

Martell, Terrence F., and Robert L. Fitts. "ERISA: Determinants of Bank Trust Usage." *Journal of Bank Research*, Spring 1978.

Schaefer, Jeffrey M., and Adolphe J. Warner. "Concentration Trends and Competition in the Securities Industry." *Financial Analysts Journal*, November/December 1977, pp. 29–34.

Shostack, G. Lynn, "Breaking Free from Product Marketing." *Journal of Marketing." Journal of Marketing*, April 1977, pp. 73–80.

Stetson, Charles P. "The Reshaping of Corporate Financial Services." *Harvard Business Review*, September-October 1980, pp. 134–42.

Strode, Thomas B., and Herman L. Lodde, Jr. "Trust Officers Sell Ideas that Solve the Customers' Problems." *Journal of Bank Research*, March 1978.

"The Future of the Financial Services Industry." *Financial Analysts Journal*, July/August 1982.

Swinyard, William R., "Strategy Development with Importance/Performance Analysis." Winter 1980, pp. 229–34.

Winton, D. S., and E. H. Nelson. "Launching New Financial Services." *Journal of the Market Research Society* 20(1).

PRIVATE AND TRADE ASSOCIATION PUBLICATIONS

"Annual Investment Performance Survey 1981." A. S. Hansen & Co., Chicago, Ill.

Christophe, Cleveland A. "Competition in Financial Services." Private paper published by First National City Corporation, March 1974.

"Facts Book," *New York Stock Exchange*, 1982 and earlier editions.

Johnson, Alfred P. "Selling Mutual Funds in Today's Market." Paper presented at Investment Dealers' Digest San Francisco Conference, Investment Company Institute, Washington D. C., November 8, 1976.

"Marketing Securities to the Small Investor." A Report to Member Organizations, prepared by Market Facts, Inc. for the New York Stock Exchange, based on survey conducted in 1971-72.

"Money Market Funds; Interested Investors and Purchasers." Prepared by Research Department, Investment Company Institute, Washington, D. C., July 1980.

"Mutual Fund Fact Book," *Investment Company Institute*, Washington, D. C., 1982.

"Mutual Funds Forum." Quarterly reviews published by Investment Company Institute, Washington, D. C., 1975–1982.

"Old Bank Robbers' Guide to Where the New Money Is," Citibank booklet published in 1981.

"Perspective on Mutual Fund Activity." Research Department, Investment Company Institute, Washington, D. C., February 1980 and Spring 1982.

"Public Attitudes toward Investing." *New York Stock Exchange*, June 1978.

"Shareownership 1981." New York Stock Exchange, April 1982.

"1982 Savings and Loan Sourcebook," *United States League of Savings Institutions*, Chicago, Ill.

"Securities Industry Trends." A periodic analysis of emerging trends in the securities industry produced by the Research Department of the Securities Industry Association, New York, N. Y., 1975–1982.

"Survey of Working Women," *Investment Company Institute*, April 1979.

"The Future of the Financial Service Industry." A private study conducted by the Hudson Institute, New York, 1982.

"The Public's Attitudes toward Mutual Funds-Awareness, Ownership and Opinions." A quantitative study prepared by National Analysts, Inc. for the Investment Company Institute, Washington, D. C., March 1971.

"The Retirement Plan Market-A Survey," *Investment Company Institute*, June 1980.

GOVERNMENT PUBLICATIONS

"Commission Rate Trends, 1975-81." Prepared by the Directorate of Economics and Policy Analysis, Securities and Exchange Commission, Washington, D. C., July 7, 1982.

"Federal Reserve Bulletin," *Board of Governors of Federal Reserve System*, 1975-83.

"Financial Institutions in a Revolutionary Era." Committee on Banking, Finance and Urban Affairs, House of Representatives, 97th Congress, 1st Session, U. S. Government Printing Office, October 1981.

NEWSPAPER ARTICLES

"American Industry Faces Huge Capital Investment to Increase Efficiency," *The New York Times*, January 11, 1981.

"Brokerage Houses Didn't Fare Well in Survey of 1982 Performance of Investment Advisers," Gary Putka, *Wall Street Journal*, January 10, 1983.

"Financial Futures Surge as Banks, Industrial Firms Move into Market," *Wall Street Journal*, March 23, 1982.

"Financial Services Get New Scrutiny," *The New York Times*, January 28, 1983.

"GE Credit: Financial Hybrid," *The New York Times*, October 8, 1981.

"Money Inc.-Wall Street Merger May Basically Change U. S. Financial System," *Wall Street Journal*, April 22, 1981.

"Regional Banks Search for a Niche in Face of New Rules, Competition," *Wall Street Journal*, February 4, 1982.

"Thrift Units Beginning to Offer Stock Services," *The New York Times*, November 8, 1982.

"Venture Capital Lures Old-Line Investment Banks," *The New York Times*, November 7, 1982.

Index

About the Author

Dr. Robert C. Perez has spent his entire career in the financial service field as a marketing professional and vice-president of F. Eberstadt & Co., Inc., a major New York investment banking and money management firm. Dr. Perez has taught marketing and finance courses at the Fordham, Baruch (CUNY), and Pace schools of business administration. He currently teaches at Iona College, Hagan School of Business Administration in New Rochelle, N. Y. Dr. Perez received his doctorate in finance from New York University Graduate School of Business Administration. His doctoral dissertation analyzed the mutual fund distribution system and spurred a number of doctoral research efforts in the emerging field of investment management marketing. Dr. Perez has appeared as an expert witness at hearings before the Securities and Exchange Commission on mutual fund distribution. In addition, he has conducted seminars here and abroad and written articles on mutual fund distribution. He conducts a private marketing consulting business in the financial service field.